Measuring the quality of care for older people

Prepared by the Clinical Effectiveness and Evaluation Unit of the Royal College of Physicians

Edited by

Jonathan Potter
Consultant Physician in Geriatric Medicine, Nunnery Fields Hospital, Canterbury
Associate Director, Clinical Effectiveness and Evaluation Unit,
Royal College of Physicians

Andrew Georgiou
Outcomes Programme Co-ordinator, Clinical Effectiveness and Evaluation Unit,
Royal College of Physicians

Michael Pearson
Director, Clinical Effectiveness and Evaluation Unit,
Royal College of Physicians

ROYAL COLLEGE OF PHYSICIANS

2000

Acknowledgements

This publication is based upon a conference held at the Royal College of Physicians on 10 November 1999, held jointly by the Clinical Effectiveness and Evaluation Unit and the National Centre for Health Outcomes Development. We would particularly like to thank Luna Islam who played an important part in organising the conference and administering the work required to produce this publication and Barbara Durr whose help in the production process was greatly appreciated.

Cover photograph: Ulrike Preuss

Royal College of Physicians of London
11 St Andrews Place, London NW1 4LE

Registered Charity No. 210508

Copyright © 2000 Royal College of Physicians of London

ISBN 1 86016 1383

Typeset by Dan-Set Graphics, Telford, Shropshire
Printed in Great Britain by Sarum ColourView Group, Salisbury, Wiltshire

Contributors

Sheila Adam
Health Services Director, NHS Executive

Iain Carpenter
Senior Lecturer, Centre for Health Services Studies, University of Kent at Canterbury/ Department of Health Care of the Elderly, Guy's, Kings and St Thomas' Medical School, London; Honorary Consultant, Kent & Canterbury Hospital, Canterbury

James Coles
Director, CASPE Research

Andrew Georgiou
Outcomes Programme Co-ordinator, Clinical Effectiveness and Evaluation Unit, Royal College of Physicians, London

Luna Islam
Project Co-ordinator, Clinical Effectiveness and Evaluation Unit, Royal College of Physicians, London

Peter Littlejohns
Clinical Director, National Institute for Clinical Excellence

Jonathan Mant
Senior Lecturer, University of Birmingham

Alastair Mason
Consultant Epidemiologist, National Centre for Health Outcomes Development

Michael Pearson
Director, Clinical Effectiveness and Evaluation Unit, Royal College of Physicians, London

Ian Philp
Co-chair, External Reference Group, National Service Framework for older people, Professor of Healthcare for older people

Jonathan Potter
Associate Director, Clinical Effectiveness and Evaluation Unit, Royal College of Physicians, London

Anthony Rudd

Associate Director, Clinical Effectiveness and Evaluation Unit, Royal College of Physicians, London

Foreword

High quality health care is the ethical responsibility of all professionals and is embedded within the Charter of both the Royal College of Physicians and the British Geriatrics Society. However, recent years have seen the need to be explicit about what is meant by the quality of care so as to enable professionals to better monitor its provision across the health service.

There is an urgent need to develop and refine relevant clinical measures that can be used for monitoring the quality of care. But defining quality is difficult. Various attempts to produce markers of quality of care have met with limited success and enthusiasm. NHS produced 'league tables of results' have either lacked the sophistication to reflect local differences, or have reflected organisational factors of limited clinical significance.

These issues are particularly important for older people. Fifty percent of the cost of the NHS is devoted to the care of older people. The introduction of the National Service Framework of Older People is itself recognition of the importance of care for older people. Crucial national issues with a bearing on older people have also arisen with the National Beds Enquiry, The Royal Commission on Long Term Care and such documents as the Department of Health Guidance on Good Practice in Continence Services.

The Royal College of Physicians and the British Geriatrics Society have long promoted high quality care for older people as part of their core activities. Recent examples include the pioneering work of Dr Anthony Hopkins within the Research Unit (now the Clinical Effectiveness and Evaluation Unit – CEEU) at the Royal College of Physicians, in developing the concept of audit and publishing extensively in this regard on a wide range of clinical conditions related to older people, along with Professor John Brocklehurst – former President of the British Geriatrics Society and Associate Director of the CEEU – who has made a major contribution to the provision and monitoring of care for older people in long term care settings.

This book arises from a conference that set out to examine how existing work might be applied to the newly announced National Service Framework for Older People. It marks an important addition to the debate around the measurement of the quality of care. It helps to map the path towards the identifying of the most appropriate methods to provide the information required, and also how that information should be made available so that it is understandable, relevant and accepted as reliable to clinicians, health managers and the public. Clinicians and managers need such information to ensure that their efforts are being used to the greatest effect and older people have a right to know that their NHS care is of a high and consistent quality.

Professor Sir George Alberti
President,
Royal College of Physicians of London

Dr Brian Williams
President,
The British Geriatrics Society

Contents

SECTION 1: INTRODUCTION

SECTION 2: THE NATIONAL AGENDA

SECTION 3: QUALITY OF CARE STUDIES

SECTION 4: DISCUSSION AND CONCLUSION

The Clinical Effectiveness and Evaluation Unit (CEEU)

The Clinical Effectiveness and Evaluation Unit of the Royal College of Physicians concentrates on those issues that are at the centre of the national healthcare agenda, eg the National Service Frameworks in Cardiology, Care of Older People and Diabetes, and the Calman-Hine Cancer Framework, as a continuous programme of work rather than multiple one-off projects. Associate Directors, who are active clinicians in their field, lead the relevant programmes in conjunction with the Director. CEEU has expertise in the development of guidelines, the organising and reporting of multi-centre comparative audit to encourage guideline implementation, and studies on how the outcome of care can be measured reliably. All work is collaborative with relevant specialist societies, patient groups and health service bodies such as the National Service Frameworks, National Institute for Clinical Excellence (NICE) and, in future, with the Centre for Health Improvement (CHI). CEEU is self-financing with funding coming from government, charities and other organisations.

Editors' Preface

The quality of care provided for older people currently gives rise to considerable concern. There has been documented evidence of inadequacies in the access to care, the standards of care and the environment within which it is provided. In response to these concerns, new national procedures have recently been announced for setting standards and measuring performance.

Against this background, the Clinical Effectiveness and Evaluation Unit (CEEU) of the Royal College of Physicians of London hosted a conference on 10 November 1999, entitled 'Measuring the quality of care for older people – preparing for the National Service Framework'. The aims of the conference were threefold:

1 To enable those working at the forefront of developing healthcare policy for older people to present details of the recent NHS initiatives to improve the healthcare for older people.

2 To present three studies undertaken by the CEEU which exemplify differing approaches to measuring the quality of care. The studies in fractured femur, stroke and urinary incontinence are particularly relevant to older people.

3 To highlight the real issues and concerns experienced by those working with older people, and, in anticipation of the National Service Framework (NSF) for older people, provide a medium by which dialogue and communication could take place between policy makers and those working on the ground.

The conference was well attended by a wide range of healthcare professionals, including managers, academics, clinicians and public health workers. The mix of professional groups ensured lively discussion periods which voiced many of the concerns and experiences of those working at the coal-face.

The first two sections of the conference provided an opportunity for key speakers who are leading the new NHS quality agenda to detail the evolving arrangements. Sheila Adam outlined the national background against which the government's new plans had been introduced, and stressed the importance of developing programmes that are both ambitious and realistic in their scope. This means ensuring the resources are available when required. Ian Philp elaborated on how the NSF for older people was carrying out its work. It aims to cover about half of the spectrum of care covered by the NHS, with a focus on the care of the frailer groups of the community. He outlined the organising principles of the External Reference Group which aims to promote health and well-being, ensure the systematic assessment of health, enhance fairness, and eliminate discrimination.

Peter Littlejohns described the role of the National Institute for Clinical Excellence as a special health authority that provides guidance on the clinical and cost effectiveness of clinical interventions. James Coles explored the issues involved in measuring and implementing quality of healthcare standards. Factors that stimulate and support change include the need to secure agreement and professional consonance in a developmental and supportive environment.

Section 3 focused on three studies undertaken by the CEEU measuring the quality of care in the areas of fractured femur, stroke and urinary incontinence.

Alastair Mason presented data on fractured femur derived from hospital episodes from the Oxford Record Linkage Study (ORLS) project. Anthony Rudd described the work of the national sentinel audit for stroke which used retrospective data gathered by audit staff from hospitals throughout the country. Jonathan Potter presented the results of a study of incontinence based on data collected by staff involved in the care of individual patients at ward, nursing home and residential home level.

The discussion sessions (summarised in Section 4) that followed each of the speakers explored issues and concerns about the national strategy. Anxieties were expressed about the emphasis on cost effectiveness rather than purely clinical effectiveness, the need for additional resources and the implications for accountability. Equally, however, there was a sense of pragmatic realism towards the importance of reflecting on current practice and aiming for improvements in efficiency without necessarily incurring increased costs. Increased public awareness of performance is both reasonable and inevitable, but requires consultation and collaboration to ensure that the demands of central control take into account the limitations implicit in setting standards and measuring the quality of care.

Discussion during the conference also reflected on the methodological difficulties associated with the setting of quality standards and the measuring of the quality of care. The setting of standards is currently founded on research-based evidence, but the inclusion and exclusion criteria of such studies may limit the application of their findings. Older people have been underrepresented in research studies, they are characterised by a high frequency of comorbidity, and are cared for in very varied settings and ways. Such issues mean that evidence-based standard setting is often difficult to accomplish.

Potential ways forward for the measurement of the quality of care include an emphasis on the use of process measures rather than outcome measures, and on the use of standardised assessment and aggregated databases. Process measures largely get round the difficulties of case mix, statistical power and confounding variables which severely limit the use of outcome measures in older people. However, there are also difficulties here:

- the process under consideration may have been carried out but not recorded
- data can be hard to collect retrospectively from records, and
- there may be significant variability between sites due to the imprecise definition and interpretation of terms by different assessors.

Such difficulties can be overcome, but they currently limit the acceptability of such data in routine practice.

The use of standardised assessment and aggregated databases has been successful in other countries and has resulted in improvements in the quality of care. Such approaches can achieve systematic assessment of individuals, standardisation of care management and the facilitation of audit, comparison and research. The diversity of practice throughout the regions makes such an approach difficult, but its implementation in specific settings (eg nursing and residential homes) might demonstrate that there are potential benefits.

A further important area of discussion addressed the methods by which changes of practice can be achieved to ensure the improvement of quality. There was a strong belief that a top down approach was needed, be it centrally or professionally driven, to ensure clinical practices changed for the better. There was a recognition that education and training programmes had often failed to deliver improved quality of care. Such an approach corresponds with the developing central agenda for setting standards and monitoring performance, and reflects a level of frustration with the inadequacies in the standards of care presently provided.

While the conference highlighted some major concerns about the far-reaching changes aimed at establishing centrally driven control over the quality of care for older people, there was also a keen awareness of the great variations, and often inadequacies, in the quality of care provided. The drive to improve quality of healthcare can proceed only through partnership. There must be recognition centrally that there are serious limitations in the current methodologies for assessing and comparing quality of care; equally, professionals have to work to develop mechanisms that are acceptable and that provide a valid reflection of the quality of care older people are entitled to expect.

JONATHAN POTTER
MICHAEL PEARSON
ANDREW GEORGIOU

SECTION 1

Introduction

1 | Standards of care for older people: an introduction to the issues

Jonathan Potter
Associate Director, Clinical Effectiveness and Evaluation Unit,
Royal College of Physicians, London

In 1946, Dr Marjorie Warren, the progenitor of geriatric medicine,[1-3] identified the large number of older people confined to inappropriate workhouse settings and denied effective healthcare. Her seminal works laid the foundation for modern improvements in medical care for older people. Over two decades later in 1969, the Health Advisory Service (HAS) was established following major concerns about the state of care in long-stay mental institutions. Its remit was to advise on the quality of care in specific hospitals.

Recent data measuring the quality of care for older people confirm continuing severe limitations in the service provided. Long and variable waiting list times for surgery such as hip replacement and cataract extraction are recognised problems within the NHS. These delays and inequalities particularly affect older people. Comparisons between the UK and other European countries show marked differences in outcomes for coronary artery disease, cancer and stroke, all of which have high prevalence in the older population.[4-6] Recent assessments of care provided on wards carried out by Age Concern, the HAS and the Audit Commission demonstrate inadequacies in communication, dignity and privacy as well as in the access to services.[7-9]

National mechanisms for improving quality of care

The national agenda

Until recent years responsibility for the setting, maintenance and monitoring of standards has resided with the professions and the various Royal Colleges and specialist societies. The Charter of the Royal College of Physicians of London, dated 1518, includes the upholding of standards both for their own honour and for public benefit.[10] The British Geriatrics Society, founded in 1948, has in its Memorandum of Association the objective of 'improving the standards of medical care for the aged and infirm ...'.[11]

Growing pressures on the health service have however changed the national picture. Governments, not only in the UK, but in all developed countries faced with the growing costs of health services, have increasingly resorted to market orientated approaches. In addition, demographic changes and technological developments are increasing pressure on the NHS. These changes, in conjunction with the new market focused philosophies that appeared in the 1980s, proclaimed a new era of 'accountability' within the health service. The Griffiths report in 1983[12] was supposed to be the key to beginning the process. Subsequently, 'resource management' initiatives, budgetary accountability down to ward level, the purchaser/provider split, league tables and the Patient's Charter were introduced to enhance financial accountability, monitor outcomes and 'improve quality'.

The market orientated approach was never fully implemented; it foundered in part due to the difficulties of establishing and monitoring contracts. Financial management of the health service remains a challenge, but major concerns more recently have focused on clinical care, particularly as a result of several high profile instances. These factors have put quality at the top of the political agenda, and have resulted in the introduction of mechanisms to ensure high quality of care to augment the traditional role of the professions. There is now a move aimed at achieving 'consensual management', supplemented by strong central direction over the setting and monitoring of quality of care.

The government White Paper, *The new NHS: modern dependable*,[13] expressed a commitment to high quality and cost effectiveness with the following objectives:

▪ To continually improve the overall standards of clinical care.

▪ To reduce unacceptable variations in clinical practice.

▪ To ensure the best use of resources so that patients receive the greatest benefit.

▪ To achieve these objectives by setting, delivering and monitoring quality standards, and by making quality of care a *managerial responsibility* rather than just a professional commitment.

Setting the standards

The government's arrangements for ensuring quality include the establishment of two new bodies to set standards:[14]

1 The National Institute for Clinical Excellence (NICE), which will establish standards against which practice will be measured.
2 The National Service Frameworks (NSFs), which will produce authoritative guidance for achieving consistent clinical standards.

The remit for the NSFs is challenging, and offers the opportunity to introduce a level of consistency into the national picture. Stroke management provides a good example. While there is a well established evidence base for specific approaches to treatment,[15,16] nationally there is great variability in both the way treatment is provided and the outcomes from treatment.[17] The NSF for older people challenges us to define the appropriate structures and processes that should be in place within the healthcare service to provide a high quality stroke service and to identify the appropriate outcome measures to monitor service delivery.

Measuring performance

The quality of services provided will be closely monitored and will become more transparent. There will be three approaches to measuring and monitoring care:
▌ the Commission for Health Improvement
▌ the National Performance Framework, and
▌ the National Survey of Patient and User Experience.[14]

The exposure of clinical practice to public review and comparison will markedly increase. While this is appropriate, it places great emphasis on ensuring that data collected reflect practice accurately and reliably, and that comparisons between different parts of the country are reasonable. It will be of the utmost importance to define all the factors that influence the service provided to patients.

Clinical implications

Clinicians will welcome the change of emphasis from 'business efficiency' to 'clinical effectiveness'. However, many questions are raised by the new proposals that require resolution:
▌ What is quality?
▌ Who defines quality?
▌ From whose perspective is quality being considered: that of the NHS, the management, the patient or the clinician?

- How is quality measured and compared?
- Are there sound methods for measuring quality?
- Will resources match the requirements to provide high quality care?

Professionals will welcome the ability to assess and monitor the quality of care provided by their service, but the current arrangements also call for some caution. Increased public awareness of differences in performance between clinical services and the managerial responsibility for the quality of care both have important implications for clinicians. It is precisely *because* quality will be identified as the responsibility of an individual that robust measurement systems are essential. People may react defensively to ensure that their responsibility is discharged, to the detriment of developing the service as a whole. In the past, there has been much scepticism of measurements such as league tables. It is therefore important to restore the confidence in and acceptance of quality measurement among professional groups, and to prove and promote the understanding that measurement can be both reliable and constructive. The ownership of data generated from quality measurement also needs to be considered – inappropriate access to data could have deleterious effects. The success of confidential enquiries is based on the sensitive handling of information.

The resource implication associated with achieving quality standards also needs to be addressed. On the one hand, there is pressure to deliver quality standards within current resources and, on the other, systems and services are already stretched to the limit and cannot go further without more input. Human resources are needed if the drive for a quality service is to have meaning. Allowance must be made in people's working time for activities such as training and maintaining lifelong learning and teaching.

Measuring quality properly cannot be performed without an adequate infrastructure that includes information technology and support personnel to collect, code, collate and disseminate data. Furthermore, measurement of quality is an ongoing process. Standards for providing care are constantly changing as new evidence and new interventions become available. Standards need to be regularly reviewed and renewed, and the processes for measurement continually maintained.

Quality is dependent on a wide range of interrelated factors, many of which are outside the control of professionals working in the health system. In measuring quality, it is important to identify and recognise the relevant factors that are not, or cannot be measured. Unless this is recognised, the credibility of any quality assurance system will be undermined.

The pursuit of quality standards using laid down guidelines may restrict professional freedom to the detriment of individual patient care.

Professionals may feel that they have to be seen to conform to guidelines, even if the individual circumstances of a patient do not conform to national norms. Innovation and enterprise may be stifled because new ideas and approaches will be seen not to conform to established practice, and may therefore be outside quality guidelines.

There is concern that centrally driven control of quality assessment associated with individual accountability will lead to a damaging culture of blame. Mechanisms need to be in place to encourage and reward the pursuit of high quality of care as well as to identify and rectify poor quality.

Any national measurements of quality that are to be made public must be based on sound methodologies, with a clear understanding of the appropriate outcomes to be measured, together with a recognition of the difficulties in collecting and interpreting data derived from different settings. This requires an understanding of the confounding factors that make interpretation of comparisons difficult. Such methodological correctness is essential if confidence is to exist in published results, and if there is to be an acceptance of corrective measures where differences are found.

Quality of care

Definitions

Donabedian has defined quality as the degree of conformance to, or deviation from, normative behaviour.[18] An alternative definition derived from Brook and Kosecoff defines quality succinctly as 'doing the right things … well'.[19,20] Both definitions identify the need to determine a standard (normative behaviour/the right thing). Measurement of quality of care can then be achieved by measuring the conformance/deviation from the standard to determine whether care was provided 'well'.

These definitions can be applied to various aspects of service. People admitted to hospital will want to know that both the clinical care and the manner in which it is given are of high quality. Donabedian recognised this when he indicated that quality of care is dependent on both 'technical care' and 'interpersonal care'.[18] Maxwell defined in more detail the aspects of care that should be considered, and identified six areas: effectiveness, efficiency, equity, social acceptability, accessibility and relevance.[21] Scally and Donaldson refined these aspects of care into the categories of professional performance (technical quality), resource use (efficiency), risk management (the risk of injury or illness associated with the service provided), and patient satisfaction.[22]

Aspects to be measured

Before defining the most appropriate approach to measuring quality, it is important to consider the aspects to be measured in more detail. The approach to measurement may well differ for different aspects of care.

Effectiveness

Care should result in the best possible health outcome, enhancing recovery, preventing deterioration, or enabling the best possible quality of life despite irremediable disease.

Are older people receiving effective care? Therein lies the challenge. Much practice to date has been determined by historical habit rather than sound evidence. Increasingly, efforts are being made to ensure that effective care is determined by sound evidence: by meta-analyses of randomised studies, single randomised studies, and by expert informed opinion. However, older people are often excluded from clinical studies, and individual patients do not necessarily conform to those entered into studies. The methodologies, inclusion and exclusion criteria of studies vary greatly, making pooling of data complex. It can be difficult to develop evidence-based recommendations for the effective care of older people. Without clear standards for care, it is not possible to measure the quality of care being provided. For many aspects of care for older people, there is still a need to determine evidence-based standards against which the effectiveness of care can be measured.

Efficiency

A major theme throughout the new proposals for quality in the NHS is to ensure both value for money and that treatment is cost effective as well as clinically effective.

The NHS, like all healthcare systems worldwide, is faced with cost control. Value for money issues have to be considered. Drug prescribing must be regularly reviewed to ensure both drug use and the method of administration are reasonable. The cost effectiveness of some drugs may need careful consideration. Zanamivir is an antiviral agent that has been shown to limit the duration of influenzal viral attack. Such a treatment may well be beneficial for at-risk groups such as older people but, according to NICE, the evidence of benefit is still lacking and there may be risks of increasing exposure to viral infections. For this reason, NICE has decided that the drug it is not currently advised as being cost effective.[23,24]

Equity

There are continuing concerns about the access of older people to medical services and treatment.[7,25] The situation has improved – indeed, one of the successes of geriatric medicine has been to contribute to ensuring enhanced access for older people to appropriate treatment and investigation. On a statistical basis, it is now recognised that for many conditions older people stand to benefit more from interventions than younger people. Because of the high frequency of illness in older people, the number needed for treatment in order to obtain benefit tends to be considerably fewer than in younger people (eg treatment of hypertension, thrombolysis in myocardial infarction [MI]).[26,27]

Social acceptability

Issues of dignity, privacy and communication are of particular importance. Older people are frequently beset with cognitive disorders and sensory problems of hearing and vision, and are often the least able to represent themselves to ensure adequate and appropriate conditions of care. They are often affected by social prejudices, express low expectations of what can be done for them, and they themselves frequently explain ill health on the basis of 'just old age'. It is important that older people recognise that much can be done to enhance their degree of independence and quality of life, and that they have an equal entitlement to quality healthcare.

Services directed towards older people should always aim to ensure socially acceptable care. The old workhouses, so long utilised to provide medical care for older people, were poor quality. Fortunately, such services have largely given way to more appropriately designed buildings and facilities. Staff attitudes towards care should constantly be promoted to ensure privacy, dignity, representation and effective communication. Once again, there continues to be evidence that the service provided for older people does not reach the quality they desire and expect.[9]

Accessibility

Questions of accessibility may refer to physical difficulties of access to facilities or to organisational difficulties older people confront with waiting lists and waiting times.[28] This is another important aspect of quality for older people. Their functional abilities and limitations make it more difficult for them to access care, and these obstacles must be resolved. One patient was sent to a hospital 80 miles from his home by a fundholding general practitioner to bypass the local waiting list for hip replacement. Despite persisting pain, the patient was unable to attend for follow-up, being so daunted by the M25 motorway that he could not make the journey. Care for older people should be local and accessible.

Waiting times remain unacceptably long. By having to wait many months for such interventions as hip replacements and cataract removal, older people suffer a double burden both in terms of quality of life and in functional limitation. In the case of cancer, the recognition that suspected cases should be seen rapidly by specialist services emphasises the importance of access to services in ensuring high quality care.

Relevance

The care provided should be relevant for the community. This implies knowledge of the demography of a locality and assessment of public health needs. Healthcare can be targeted and prioritised to meet these needs. In areas with a high percentage of older people, particular consideration is required to ensure there are sufficient services and facilities to meet their needs. This may include strengthening the community-based services for assessment, community-based rehabilitation and support.

Approaches to measurement

In the new NHS, measurements of quality will produce information that is to be available for public scrutiny. It is essential that the professional groups providing the service are happy that their activities are fairly reflected in such measurements, which means they must be aware of the strengths and limitations of the differing measures of quality.

The challenge is to determine pragmatic measures of quality: measures that can be derived from reliable data collected routinely and accurately from clinical practice. It is not difficult subjectively to recognise good quality of care – the requirement is to find objective measures to capture such performance.

Standard setting and indicators

Selected standards can be utilised as indicators of good practice. The National Centre for Health Outcomes Development has recently used multidisciplinary working groups to generate outcome indicators for a wide range of conditions. Many of these indicators are relevant to the care of older people, and relate to conditions such as fractured femur, stroke and incontinence.[29–31]

The studies presented in Chapters 6 (fractured femur), 7 (stroke) and 9 (urinary incontinence) have evaluated the use of health outcome indicators, and discussed their strengths and weaknesses. Various factors determine the usefulness of such indicators. For example, an indicator should be relevant to the condition under consideration, understandable and acceptable. The use of indwelling catheters exemplifies a health outcome indicator for incontinence. Such a measure is clearly relevant to incontinence, and would be understandable and acceptable to practitioners managing people with incontinence. Another important aspect of an indicator is that it should be accurate and reliable. An indicator such as 'appropriate clinical examination' may lead to inaccuracy as there is no precise definition of 'appropriate'. Such imprecision is likely to lead to variation in interpretation between observers.

If suitable caution is taken in the selection of health outcome measures, they can be useful in indicating possible inadequacies in care. It should, however, be recognised that poor outcome indicator results do not inevitably imply poor care, but simply indicate where further assessment of the care should be undertaken. As shown by Alastair Mason in Chapter 6, indicators should come with a health warning: they are *indicators*, not definitive *determinants* of quality of care.

Methods for measuring quality of care

After standards have been set and indicators selected, reliable methods for the measurement of clinical practice are required. It will then be possible to compare results with the established standards, so as to determine the deviation from normative performance, as per Donabedian.[18] Many approaches have been adopted to measure quality, some of which are detailed in Table 1. Donabedian developed his views, by suggesting that quality can be measured against standards by assessing the structures, processes and outcomes associated with practice. These proposals form the basis of much current practice in quality measurement and will be considered in more detail in Chapters 6, 7 and 9. These issues were also widely referenced by delegates at the conference (see Chapter 11).

Structures

Structures, both in terms of facilities and staffing, will be more likely to deliver a high quality service if they are of an adequate quality. In many

Table 1. Approaches to measuring quality in healthcare.[19]

• Confidential inquiries
• Random notes audit
• Medical/clinical audit
• Peer review
• Questionnaire
• Complaints
• Utilisation review
• Critical incident review

ways, data about structure are the easiest to obtain, and thus are particularly attractive from a managerial viewpoint. It is straightforward to record the facilities available, the staffing numbers and skill mixes. Such data form the basis of accreditation schemes, and systems of this type are widely used internationally and in some parts of the UK as an indication of quality.

Too often, however, NHS facilities are outdated or found to be suboptimal. Good care can be provided in such settings, but often solely due to conscientious and hard-working staff. Equally, high class facilities do not guarantee premium care. Facilities have to be matched with staff who are provided with training and the expertise to carry out the appropriate care.

Process

Having set the standards of care to be achieved, these can be met if specific processes of care management are followed. In stroke care, evidence has indicated that co-ordinated, multidisciplinary care on stroke units achieves better outcomes than care on general medical wards.[32] It is reasonable to assume, therefore, that the institution of a stroke unit where it has not previously been present will result in improved standards of care. Stroke units include a wide range of processes involving nursing care (positioning, transferring of patient, bowel and bladder care) and care from therapists (swallow assessment, specialist neurophysiotherapy, occupational therapy). By measuring or recording whether such processes have occurred, it is possible to make an assessment of whether care meets a desired standard.

Process methods are attractive as a measure of quality. In pragmatic terms, it can be much easier to collect data on process than on outcomes. Process is an important determinant of quality, irrespective of the confounding influence of case mix – a major difficulty with outcome measurements. Increasing research evidence will also help to provide an indication of the process measures that are important in determining high quality care.

There are problems, however. If specific process measures are identified as the markers for quality, departments and services wishing to be seen to provide high quality care may concentrate purely on the selected process to the detriment of overall care. The process to be measured needs to be clearly defined. For example, in stroke care, a swallow assessment is important as a process measure: what is a swallow assessment, and how comprehensive should it be? To ensure reliable comparison, it will be essential that all process measures are clearly defined so that like is compared with like.[33]

Data to assess performance is usually collected retrospectively, leading to major problems of reliability:

- Is the information required in records?
- Can the recordings be read?
- Do people record the same thing in the same way?
- Can the records be found?
- A process or procedure may often be carried out but not recorded.

Indeed, there is a concern that such monitoring and measuring of quality will require every care intervention to be recorded in a consistent way. This is likely to give rise to an overwhelming load of paper work to the detriment of patient care.

Outcome

The ideal measure of quality is an 'outcome' measure:

- Does the quality of care result in outcomes that match the 'normative' standard set?
- Does the assessment and treatment of patients with incontinence, for instance, result in a reduction of the prevalence of incontinence?
- Is the resultant prevalence of incontinence at a level expected in such a population in 'normal' circumstances?

Outcomes, however, can be hard to measure. There are major problems in relating the population under consideration with the group from which the standard was determined. It is important to be clear whether the relevant outcome is being measured to reflect the patient's viewpoint or that of the clinician or management.

Does the outcome measure the desired end-point? A measure such as neurological impairment in stroke patients may be favoured by clinicians as an outcome measure, but does not necessarily reflect the handicap experienced by a patient. It is the *handicap* associated with stroke that is likely to be the patient's prime concern.

Is the outcome measure a true measure or a surrogate measure? For example, measures that reflect increased bone density following treatment for osteoporosis may suggest stronger bones and less likelihood of fracture. The important outcome, however, is actual reduction in the number of fractures – a measure not so easy to obtain.

Does the population match the population on which the standard is based? The major problem with outcome measurement is that of case mix. Patients entering a service in an inner city area will differ from those in suburban and rural areas. There are likely to be differences in socio-economic class, ethnicity, affluence, social services provision, social support, etc – all of which will impact on the possible outcome of healthcare, and render comparison between such groups unreliable and misleading. For these reasons, league tables have generated some bizarrely anomalous results and are mistrusted. If public scrutiny of outcome measures is to occur, great care will be needed to adjust for the potential confounding factors.

Whilst it is valuable to delineate clearly the various dimensions of care as per Donabedian, it is also important to emphasise their inter-relationships.[34] For Hopkins,[35] the process and outcome measures of care are complementary (not competing) measures of quality. Hence, outcomes are valid only to the extent that they relate to the antecedent process of care, just as measures of the process of care are valid in so far as they relate to outcome.

Desired characteristics of measurement

The reality of busy clinical settings is that the collection of data for quality measurement is extremely difficult. To obtain data that are useful for assessing quality locally and comparatively, some specific characteristics are required.

Reliability

The usefulness of quality measures will in part depend on the reliability of their measurement. Inter-rater reliability will determine whether two independent people making the measurement produce the same result. The reliability of data may also be compared with a 'gold standard' to determine whether the person performing the measurement approximates to the 'ideal' result. In addition, it is important that the measurement is such that an assessor achieves a high level of test-retest reliability when repeating assessments over time.

It may seem reasonable to expect that different people with the same access to a data source will come up with the same results, but in reality it can be difficult to achieve. Data are collected and recorded in different ways in different settings. For example, some units and departments may have multidisciplinary notes, others will have individual notes for different professions. Some may have standardised forms, care pathways and clerking proformas, while others will rely on free text. The ability to retrieve data will also vary greatly. Relevant data may not have been measured or not recorded. These issues were highlighted by a study of clinical outcome indicators in stroke by the Clinical Effectiveness and Evaluation Unit.[33]

Coding and definitions pose further problems. The quality of care for people who have sustained a 'fall' will be an important issue being addressed by the NSF. The definition of a fall is complex[36] – an event which results in a person coming to rest inadvertently on the ground or other lower level, other than as a consequence of:

▌ sustaining a violent blow

▌ loss of consciousness

▌ sudden onset of a paralysis, or

▌ an epileptic seizure.

Different people may interpret such a definition differently. It is essential that the starting point is the same in measuring quality standards. Coding using a retrospective review of the notes can be equally difficult. An audit of patients with diabetes mellitus included three individuals with diabetes insipidus incorrectly coded (Potter JM. Personal communication). Death certification has prevailing trends (eg MI was not recognised or entered on certification in the earlier part of the 20th century). All these factors make it difficult to compare the quality of care over time.

Most quality analysis is based on retrospective data, yet such data analysis is difficult. It may not be possible to obtain all the notes, which raises the question as to whether the missing notes represent a select group. For instance, it may be more difficult to get the notes of patients who have died. Patients on anticoagulants may stop their medication for various reasons: they may cardiovert back to sinus rhythm, have complications associated with anticoagulation, be difficult to control, and/or be non-compliant. Is it possible to trace the records of all patients who have had treatment to identify the reason they have stopped?

Bias can creep in, depending on who is collecting the data. Staff involved in the care of patients being audited may have a tendency to err on the side of showing things in a good light. Audit department staff could be more independent in such circumstances.

Validity

Are the measures of quality valid? Is there evidence that the measures reflect quality, and that changes in quality of care are reflected in changes in the measures? Research evidence has demonstrated that beta-blockers provide important prophylaxis following MI.[37] Measurement of the use of beta-blockade following MI can therefore provide an indication of the quality of care for such people. If the percentage of eligible patients receiving beta-blockade rises, it is likely that the quality of care will have been improved. It is also likely that departments with a higher percentage of patients on beta-blockers will be providing a better quality of care. It is not absolute, however, because case mix issues will need to be carefully considered.

Are the quality measures measuring what is required? Research evidence indicates that stroke units improve recovery.[32] The quality of care on stroke units might therefore be measured by the degree of recovery from neurological impairment. However, a more relevant and useful measure of the quality of care will be the residual disability, as measured by how independently individuals are able to live.

Sensitivity

Is the measure of quality sensitive, given the population size being measured? For example, when assessing the management of diabetic care in older people, the reduction of vascular complications is an important target. It would be possible to count the number of patients with diabetes having amputations but, because only a few diabetics have an amputation, the measure would not detect whether the larger number of diabetics had been correctly managed at an earlier stage. It might be more appropriate to look at process measures such as palpation of pulses, measurement of vascular flow rates by Doppler or angiographic investigation. Unless the correct measure is used, it will not be possible to interpret the variations between units, and within a unit over time.

Generalisability

The use of measures should not be restricted to specific locations. Thus, in measuring the quality of care for patients with incontinence, the measures need to be equally applicable in the community, in nursing and residential home settings as well as in hospital settings. Data that depend on facilities available only in hospital limit the usefulness of the quality measure.

The measures should be acceptable to healthcare staff since it is they who are in a position to judge whether the data collected are reasonable and accurate. It is also important that they have confidence in the measures used because they are being judged by those quality measures.

Conclusion

The desire to see high standards of care for older people is shared by all healthcare professionals. The opportunity and challenges set by the establishment of the NSF for older people should be embraced as an opportunity to take forward a set of priorities that have been long overshadowed.

However the public accountability associated with the new plans means that systems for measuring, comparing and contrasting care between services must be based on truly reliable and acceptable data systems. The professionals charged with providing care must have the confidence that innovation and enterprise will continue to be rewarded and encouraged, that the complexity of healthcare is acknowledged, and that resources and skills will be made available when their need is identified. The public, too, must have confidence that the measuring systems are assessing outcomes they value, and that the data provided are being reviewed in an open manner and problems are being acted upon.

The many methodological difficulties in measuring the quality of care for older people have to be recognised, but approaches that provide an indication for the way forward are available. The studies presented in this book demonstrate many of the current strengths and weaknesses in measuring quality of care. There is an important need to develop on the strengths, so that credible data can be made available and the quality agenda be moved forward.

References

1   Warren MW. Care of the chronic aged sick. *Lancet* 1946; **i**: 841.
2   Warren MW. Geriatrics: a medical, social and economic problem. *Practitioner* 1946; **157**: 384.
3   Warren MW. Care of the chronic sick: a case for treating chronic sick in blocks in a general hospital. *Br Med J* 1943; **2**: 822.
4   Rayner M, Petersen S. *European cardiovascular disease statistics*. London: British Heart Foundation, 2000.
5   Sikora K. Cancer survival in Britain. *Br Med J* 1999; **319**: 461–2.

6   Wolfe C, Beech R, Ratcliffe M, Rudd AG. Stroke care in Europe. Can we learn lessons from the different ways stroke is managed in different countries? *J R Soc Health* 1995; **115**: 143–7.

7   Age Concern. *Turning your back on us: older people and the NHS.* London: Age Concern, 1999.

8   Health Advisory Service 2000 Report. *Not because they are old.* London: HAS, 1998.

9   Audit Commission. *The coming of age: improving care services for older people.* London: Audit Commission, 1997.

10 Jarman B. *The quality of care in hospitals.* Harveian Oration. London: Royal College of Physicians of London, 1999.

11 British Geriatrics Society. *British Geriatrics Society Handbook.* London: British Geriatrics Society, 1997.

12 DHSS: NHS Management Enquiry team. *The Griffiths Report.* National Health Service Management Enquiry. London: HMSO, 1983.

13 Department of Health. *The new NHS: modern dependable.* Cm 3807. London: HMSO, 1997.

14 Department of Health. *A first class service: quality in the new NHS.* London: HMSO, 1998.

15 Scottish Intercollegiate Guidelines Network. *A national clinical guideline recommended for use in Scotland by the Scottish Intercollegiate Guidelines Network* (SIGN). Edinburgh: SIGN, 1997.

16 *Stroke module of the Cochrane database of systematic reviews.* London: British Medical Journal Publishing, 1996.

17 Rudd A, Irwin P, Rutledge Z, Lowe D, *et al.* The national sentinel audit for stroke: a tool for raising standards of care. *J R Coll Physicians Lond* 1999; **33**: 460–4.

18 Donabedian A. The quality of care. How can it be assessed? *JAMA* 1988; **260**: 1743–8.

19 Dickinson E. The quality movement. In: Mayer P, Dickinson E, Sandler M (eds). *Quality care for elderly people.* London: Chapman & Hall Medical, 1997.

20 Brook RH, Kosecoff JB. Commentary: competition and quality. *Health Affairs* 1988; **7**: 150–61.

21 Maxwell RJ. Quality assessment in health. *Br Med J* 1984; **288**: 1470–2.

22 Scally G, Donaldson LJ. The NHS's 50 Anniversary. Clinical governance and the drive for quality improvement in the New NHS in England. *Br Med J* 1998; **317**: 61–5.

23 Zanamivir for influenza. *Drug Ther Bull* 1999; **37**: 81–4.

24 Chief Medical Officer's Update 24. *NICE's guidance on the use of zanamivir (Relenza) for the treatment of influenza.* London: Department of Health, December 1999.

25 Bowling A. Ageism in cardiology. *Br Med J* 1999; **319**: 1353–5.

26 Mulrow CD, Cornell JA, Herrera CR. Hypertension in the elderly. Implications and generalizability of randomized trials. *JAMA* 1994; **272**: 1932–8.

27 Baillie SP, Furniss SS. Thrombolysis for elderly patients – which way from here? *Age Ageing* 1991; **20**: 1–2.

28 Turner-Stokes L, Turner-Stokes T, Schon K, Turner-Stokes H, *et al.* Charter for disabled people using hospitals: a completed access audit cycle. *J R Coll Physicians Lond* 2000; **34**: 185–9.

29 Rudd A, Goldacre M, Amess M, Fletcher J, *et al* (eds). *Health outcome indicators: stroke. Report of a working group to the Department of Health.* Oxford: National Centre for Health Outcomes Development, 1999.

30   Fairbank J, Goldacre M, Mason A, Wilkinson E, *et al* (eds). *Fractured proximal femur. Report of a working group to the Department of Health.* Oxford: National Centre for Health Outcomes Development, 1999.

31   Brocklehurst J, Amess M, Goldacre M, Mason A, *et al* (eds). *Health outcome indicators for urinary incontinence. Report of a working group to the Department of Health.* Oxford: National Centre for Health Outcomes Development, 1999.

32   Stroke Unit Trialists' Collaboration. *Organised in-patient (stroke unit) care for stroke* (Cochrane Review). In: The Cochrane Library, Issue 4, 1999. Oxford: Software Update.

33   Rudd A, Pearson M, Georgiou A (eds). *Measuring clinical outcomes in stroke (acute care).* London: Royal College of Physicians, 2000.

34   Georgiou A. Health outcome indicators for asthma using patient-assessed impact measures. In: Pearson MG, Bucknall CE (eds). *Measuring clinical outcome in asthma: a patient-focused approach.* London: Royal College of Physicians, 1999.

35   Hopkins A. *Measuring the quality of medical care.* London: Royal College of Physicians, 1990.

36   Kellogg international work group on the prevention of falls in the elderly. The prevention of falls in later life. *Dan Med Bull* 1987; **34** (Suppl 4): 1–24.

37   Yusuf S, Peto R, Lewis J, Collins R, *et al.* Beta blockade during and after myocardial infarction: an overview of the randomised trials. *Prog Cardiovasc Dis* 1985; **27**: 335–71.

SECTION 2

The National Agenda

2 | Establishing national standards and defining service models in health and social care for older people

Sheila Adam
Health Services Director, NHS Executive

There are two important reasons for focusing one of the earliest National Service Frameworks (NSFs) on older people. Older people are major users of health and social services and also of a number of other public services, and their number will rise over the next 10 years. Those of us who are part of the post-war baby boom will be boosting the numbers of older people over about the next 20 years. It is not surprising, therefore, that there is considerable public concern to ensure that the services provided for older people continue to improve.

Dealing with areas of public concern

One of the issues of concern when the NSF was set up was the reports in the national press, documenting some worrying incidences of NHS failure to provide the rounded care on acute wards that older people frequently need. There are also major concerns about premature discharge from hospital. Discharge planning has been talked about a lot over about the last five years, but it is not always being delivered on the ground. Discharge is not always being planned from the time of admission, and there are still too many examples of older people being discharged without staff being able to make all the necessary arrangements. Another important issue that will be addressed through the NSF is that of patients being denied treatment on the grounds of age, anecdotal examples of which are provided in the Age Concern report.[1] Finally, there are geographical variations in the care of older people.

What the National Service Frameworks will include

The government is committed to addressing the issue of inequalities both in health and in the delivery of healthcare. The NSF will tackle variations and drive up quality. *A first class service*[2] set out a quality framework for health services made up of three components (Table 1):

1 Standards will be set by the NSFs and the National Institute for Clinical Excellence through appraisals of new technologies, and also through clinical guidelines and clinical audit methodologies.

2 There will be local delivery systems for quality, particularly using the framework of clinical governance within NHS organisations, linking the strands of continuous quality improvement to professional self-regulation and lifelong learning.

3 There will be monitoring arrangements to assess progress and to ensure that problems are identified and addressed, and that lessons are learnt.

Table 1. Components of the National Service Frameworks.

- national standards and service models
- underpinning programmes
- delivery strategy
- milestones and performance indicators

One of the traditional criticisms of both the Department of Health and the NHS is that we are better at saying what we are going to do than in ensuring that the necessary progress is made. NHS performance used to be seen predominantly in terms of financial performance and activity. The new Performance Assessment Framework has six domains, including clinical effectiveness, health outcomes and – importantly – the patient/carer experience. The fact that the outcome might look fine from the point of view of professionals must be balanced by how it is seen and felt by patients and their families. The Commission for Health Improvement, now being established, will have a number of functions. It will visit each NHS organisation over a four-year cycle, and take a specific interest in clinical governance and in the implementation of NSFs. There is also the National Patient Survey, a programme of surveys beginning to unfold. The first was on patients' experience of using their general practitioner (GP) services. This will be followed by heart disease, with plans beyond that to focus on other NSF topics. The surveys will establish national benchmarks of people's experience of the services we are all striving to improve.

Requirements for delivering National Service Frameworks

The purpose of NSFs is to drive up quality in healthcare. They will be challenging, requiring critical evaluation to ensure effective and timely delivery. The NSFs will contribute towards delivering the three White Papers, not only *The new NHS*[3] but also *Modernising social services*[4] and *Our healthier nation*.[5]

NSFs will cover the spectrum of health from health promotion, disease prevention, diagnosis, assessment, treatment, care, and where appropriate, palliative care. The criteria for selecting an NSF are shown in Table 2. The NSF programme, which builds on the Calman-Hine report[6] on cancer services and on paediatric intensive care, is given in Table 3. Much has been learnt from the process of implementing this report. The work on the mental health NSF (published in 1999), which focused on working age adults, has been intensive and sought to integrate the knowledge base with clear proposals for implementation. The NSF on coronary heart disease is to be followed by NSFs on older people and diabetes. All the NSFs will incorporate a series of national standards and service models, and include some underpinning programmes to support local implementation. This is an area where they diverge from the Calman-Hine[6] approach. They will discuss delivery strategies, and include some milestones and performance indicators.

Consistent themes underpin the NSF programmes:

▌ What are the key standards and service models?

Table 2. Criteria for selecting a National Service Framework.

- relevance to wider government agenda
- important issues in terms of mortality, morbidity, disability or resource use
- area of public concern
- evidence of shortfall between actual and acceptable practice
- complex care pathways
- need for service improvement requiring major reconfiguration
- need for new and innovative approaches

Table 3. The National Service Framework (NSF) programme.

Specialty covered	Date of completion
Mental health	September 1999
Coronary heart disease	March 2000
Older people	2000
Diabetes	2001

▌ What are the knowledge gaps?
▌ What needs to be prioritised in research and development?
▌ How can clinicians be supported in making evidence-based decisions?

An example is some interesting current work drawing up referral guidelines for GPs for patients who may have cancer. There is a target that by the end of 2000, patients whose GP suspects cancer will be seen by a specialist within two weeks. It is important that support is provided to GPs in making the referral decision. When groups of experts get together on cancer, they learn from each other, and it is essential to interpret the knowledge base and make it as accessible and user-friendly as possible for GPs. There is great potential here as we begin to develop better electronic methods, but in some areas we will have to start with paper-based systems.

Clinical information incorporating clinical data sets will be critical in implementing all the NSFs. Mike Richards, the National Cancer Director, has already prioritised information as one of his most important tasks. A similar priority applies to human resources. Even if the money is available, factors that will become increasingly important are:

▌ Do we have the people we need?
▌ Are they working in the right way?
▌ Do they have the necessary skills?
▌ Are they good at teamworking?
▌ Can they work across boundaries?

Where standards and milestones require additional resources, there is an obvious need to ensure that the evidence informs decisions about further expenditure. Public expenditure is now planned on a three-year basis. At a local level, all the levers need to be incorporated, from health improvement programmes through long-term service agreements, clinical governance, partnerships and the local development plans which are coming together around each NSF as it is published.

In summary, if NSFs are to be delivered, programmes will be needed that are ambitious but which realistically focus on a small number of priorities. We need to secure change in the short term, as well as ensuring that the long-term strategic change is sustainable.

References

1   Age Concern. *Turning your back on us: older people and the NHS.* London: Age Concern, 1999.
2   Department of Health. *A first class service: quality in the new NHS.* London: HMSO, 1998.

3   Department of Health. *The new NHS: modern, dependable.* Cm 3807. London: HMSO, 1997.

4   Secretary of State for Health. *Modernising social services: promoting independence, improving protection, raising standards.* Cm 4169. London: HMSO, 1998.

5   Secretary of State for Health. *Our healthier nation: a contract for health.* Cm 4386. London: HMSO, 1998.

6   Calman K, Hine D. A policy framework for commissioning cancer services. A report by the Expert Advisory Group on Cancer to the Chief Medical Officers of England and Wales. London: Department of Health, 1995.

3 | The National Service Framework for NHS care of older people and the role of the External Reference Group

Ian Philp
Co-chair, External Reference Group, National Service Framework for older people,
Professor of Healthcare for older people

Most of us who have chosen to work with older people are often asked the reasons. Three things come to mind:

1 This is where the greatest need lies and the greatest opportunity exists to make a difference in healthcare today.

2 Geriatric medicine requires humanity, and bestows the pleasure of working with people in a way that sustains both the patients' and our own humanity.

3 Geriatric medicine is one of the specialties that allows us to work with colleagues from different backgrounds and disciplines for the care of our patients.

The National Service Framework (NSF) provides an opportunity to celebrate excellent practice, to increase levels up to the good practice that exists in most of the country, and to make all practice better. This chapter will address what is covered in the NSF for the care of older people, how the External Reference Group (ERG) has gone about its work, and what might be the impact of the NSF.

It is important to highlight some of the NSF constraints:

1 NSFs cover NHS care in England only, and may or may not be followed by the other countries of the UK.

2 The NSF for NHS care of older people is about reorganising care within existing resources and planned growth in resources.

3 The ERG is advising government, *not* writing the NSF. One of the aims of the ERG is to try to ensure that something is produced that will make a big difference and be acceptable to government.

This NSF will cover approximately half of the spectrum of activities covered by the NHS. It has a particular focus on the frailer and oldest groups within the population. The importance of the promotion of both health and well-being for all older people is not being forgotten, and there are implications in the NSF for their promotion for younger and fitter older people as well as for frailer older people. The NSF not only covers NHS care for all older people, but also looks at all adults with stroke, falls and with dementia. It makes no sense to talk about an age separation at age 65 for these conditions because, while they are particularly important in old age, they also demand a response that addresses all age groups.

The care of older people with depression is also being looked at, together with the promotion of positive palliative care needs. Recommendations in the area of palliative care cover not only those traditionally associated with specialist palliative care services (older people dying of cancer and other terminal illnesses) but also general issues both about end of life care for older people and about the relief of distressing symptoms of old age, not necessarily associated with a terminal illness. Effective healthcare cannot be delivered to older people unless the work is carried out closely with social services. This key relationship is reflected in the ERG, whose co-chair is Denise Platt, Chief Inspector for Social Services.

With such a large and complex field to cover, it was important to have a small, effective and hard-working ERG which would, in turn, link to a wider community of experts, older people, families and family carers, all of whom contribute to the rich diversity of perspectives.

Task groups

Seven members of the ERG chaired task groups linked to particular aspects of the care system for older people. Three task groups worked on the conditions of stroke, falls and mental illness. Two task groups looked at NHS care for older people from the perspective of the setting of care: acute hospitals, primary care and community care. Another group looked at transitions in care both within the NHS and across into other agencies. A last task group looked into the systematic assessment and co-ordinated response to the needs of older people and the care planning process. Two ERG members represented older people and family carers. They, in turn, managed a group of older people and a group of family carers providing parallel advice. Three other ERG task group members looked at themes such as age discrimination and the need for a primary care-led NHS.

Each task group was asked to think about developing standards and indicators in their areas in relation to some organising principles, a method of working that aimed to bring coherence to the process. In addition, the task groups were asked to think about service models and implementation issues.

Organising principles

The four principles that underlie the ERG, with the aim of ensuring that older people receive the right kind of healthcare, are:

1   To promote health and well-being.
2   To ensure the systematic assessment of health and social care needs.
3   To co-ordinate the response to identified needs.
4   To tackle the issues of fairness and discrimination.

It is established policy that healthcare should be delivered solely on the basis of need but, as Age Concern has highlighted,[1] there is age discrimination in our society which is reflected to some extent in the NHS. Discrimination has many dimensions, as was apparent to the relevant task groups. Their main concern was to look at how the NHS delivers care to overcome discrimination by age, gender, race, location (including whether an old person is in a nursing home) and by disability, both physical and cognitive.

It was also important to look at how care is delivered. It is necessary to ensure that the NHS promotes the autonomy and independence of older people, and preserves their dignity. Unfortunately, there is evidence that in some places and in some circumstances the dignity of older persons is threatened. It is important to ensure that support be given to family care providers and others who undertake informal care, and that they are seen as partners in care whose own needs must also be addressed. Finally, it is essential to ensure that NHS staff are trained to be competent in caring for older people.

Standards, indicators and service models

Standards, indicators and service models that relate to the principles outlined above have been developed. It is not possible to undertake a systematic review of all aspects of NHS care of older people, but it is important to be as systematic and honest about the evidence base as possible. Members of the ERG were therefore asked to identify the key areas of concern. Extensive computer searches of the literature were conducted, from which ERG members selected the 300–400 references that they saw as key. These were then incorporated into the report, and the weight and strength of the evidence evaluated.

Conclusion

In looking at the population of older people in this country, it is essential that a key indicator of the success of the NSF is that it brings a reduction in the levels of disability, and therefore improvement in the independence of older people. However, it would also be positive if all the older people in surveys said that they have both increased expectations of the NHS and a more positive experience of care. Surveys of carers should demonstrate that they feel they are considered as genuine partners who are involved with professionals, and that their own needs are being addressed. Staff should feel that they have the necessary knowledge, skills and attitudes to deliver appropriate care – and that they are proud to work in a quality service.

This is a large and complex field which requires a sophisticated approach to improving quality. If it is done correctly, we could have a system of NHS care for older people that would be the envy of the world.

Reference

1   Age Concern. *Turning your back on us: older people and the NHS.* London: Age Concern, 1999.

4 | Promoting clinical effectiveness: the National Institute for Clinical Excellence perspective

Peter Littlejohns
Clinical Director, National Institute for Clinical Excellence

This chapter describes the role of the National Institute for Clinical Excellence (NICE) in improving clinical and cost effectiveness of the services provided by the NHS.

The government's approach to improving quality in the NHS was made explicit in the White Paper, *The New NHS: modern dependable*,[1] with further details provided in *A first class service: quality in the new NHS.*[2] Standards are to be set at a national level, but there is a recognition that the responsibility for implementation has to be at a local level. Monitoring of this process will be undertaken locally through clinical governance, and nationally by a variety of mechanisms. These include the Commission for Health Improvement set within a National Performance Framework (see Fig 1).

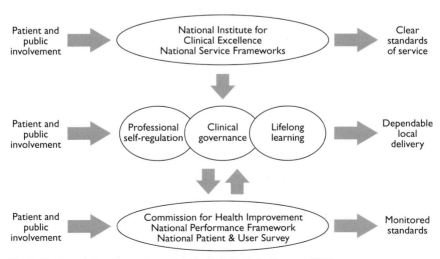

Fig 1. *Setting, delivering and monitoring standards in the new NHS.*

Setting, delivering and monitoring standards

NICE is a special health authority (SHA) established on 1 April 1999. Its role is to provide national guidance on the clinical and cost effectiveness of clinical interventions. It will achieve this through appraising new and existing technologies, developing clinical guidelines and supporting clinical audit. Details of all its activities are available on its website (www.nice.org.uk). Its specific advice will be incorporated into the broader organisational standards set by the National Service Frameworks (NSFs). It is a small organisation (about 20 employees), and undertakes its work by commissioning and liaising with a range of professional, specialist and patient organisations. It is supported by a Partners' Council, a series of advisory committees, and has formal links with a number of universities and the National Research and Development Programme (NRDP). It works closely with local trusts and clinical governance professionals to ensure support for those responsible for implementing its guidance. This includes providing audit advice to accompany its guidance.

The National Institute for Clinical Excellence approach

The main functions of NICE are listed in Table 1.

Table 1. The main functions of the National Institute for Clinical Excellence for 2000–2001.

• Appraising health technologies
• Clinical guidelines
• Referral advice
• Support of clinical audit

Appraising health technologies

The Department of Health (DoH) and the National Assembly for Wales select technologies for appraisal by NICE, based on several criteria:

1 Is the technology likely to result in a significant health benefit, taken across the NHS as a whole, if given to all patients for whom it is indicated?

2 Is the technology likely to result in a significant impact on other health-related government policies (reduction in health inequalities)?

3 Is the technology likely to have a significant impact on NHS resources (financial or other) if given to all patients for whom it is indicated?

4 Is NICE likely to be able to add value by issuing national guidance? For instance, in the absence of such guidance, is there likely to be significant controversy over the interpretation or significance of the available evidence on clinical and cost effectiveness?

NICE follows a transparent and well-structured process for its appraisals (outlined in Fig 2), giving appropriate interested parties the opportunity to submit evidence, to comment on draft conclusions, and to appeal to a panel independent of those involved in the original judgement. This is for cases in which NICE is alleged to have failed to act fairly, have exceeded its powers, or acted perversely in the light of the evidence submitted. The current form of this process is set out in NICE's 'Interim appraisal guidelines' (available on request from NICE).

NICE's function in relation to appraisals, as set out in the Secretary of State's directions, is to appraise the clinical benefits and the costs of such healthcare interventions and to make recommendations.

It assesses the evidence of all the clinical and other health-related benefits of an intervention. This is taken in its widest sense to include

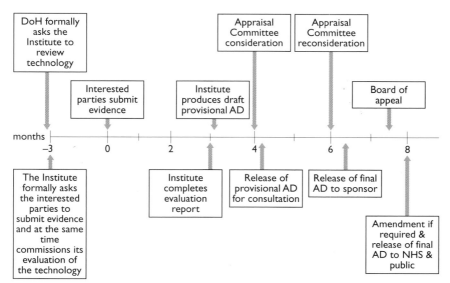

Fig 2. *Diagrammatic representation of appraisal process* (AD = appraisal determination; DoH = Department of Health).

impact on quality of life, relief of pain or disability etc, as well as any impact on likely length of life, in order to estimate the associated costs and to reach a judgement on whether, on balance, this intervention can be recommended as a cost effective use of NHS resources (in general or for specific indications, subgroups, etc). Where there is already a cost effective intervention for the condition, NICE will appraise the net impact on both benefits and costs of the new intervention relative to this benchmark.

NICE is also required to ensure that, in carrying out its statutory functions, it is sympathetic to the longer-term interest of the NHS in encouraging innovation.

Evaluation documentation is prepared by the Appraisal Secretariat or commissioned from expert groups (working closely with the Health Technology Assessment arm of the NRDP). An Appraisal Committee (Table 2) carries out the appraisals.

NICE produces guidance to commissioners and clinicians on the appropriate use of the intervention alongside current best practice. This guidance covers:

Table 2. Membership of the Appraisal Committee.

Chairman: Professor David Barnett	
Membership	No.
Vice-chairman	1
Health economists	3
Health managers	3
General practitioners	2
Hospital physicians	2
Patient advocates	2
Public health physician	1
Biostatistician	1
Community nurse	1
Hospital nurse	1
Diagnostic pathologist	1
Pharmaceutical physician	1
Pharmacist	1
Surgeon	1

* Additional *ad hoc* members may be appointed for the day by the Chairman, Vice-chairman or Chief Executive.

▌ an assessment of whether or not the intervention can be recommended as clinically effective and as a cost effective use of resources for NHS use, either in general or in particular circumstances (first- or second-line treatment, for particular subgroups, for routine use, only in the context of targeted research, etc)

▌ any priorities for treatment, where appropriate

▌ recommendations on any questions requiring further research to inform clinical practice

▌ an assessment of any wider implications for the NHS

▌ a concise summary of the reasoning behind NICE's recommendations and the evidence considered, with a supporting paper available on request.

When appropriate, NICE will also prepare guidance for users and carers, consulting with appropriate patient groups on the best format and means of dissemination. This guidance will explain the nature of the clinical recommendations, the implications for the standards which patients can expect, and the broad nature of the evidence on which the recommendations are based.

The DoH has now formally announced the first group of technologies for NICE to appraise (Tables 3 and 4).

Clinical guidelines

Academic centres, professional organisations and enthusiastic individuals in the UK have made major contributions to the production of clinical guidelines. The UK has also made a significant contribution to the

Table 3. Technologies to be appraised Autumn 1999.

- Advances in hearing aids
- Routine wisdom teeth extraction
- Liquid-based cytology
- Coronary stent developments
- Taxanes for ovarian and breast cancer
- Inhaler systems for childhood asthma (devices)
- Proton pump inhibitors for treatment of dyspepsia
- Beta-interferon/glutarimer for multiple sclerosis
- Zanamivir/oseltamivir for influenza

Table 4. Technologies to be appraised early 2000.

- Oseltamivir for influenza
- Orlistat and sibutramine for obesity
- Laparoscopic surgery
- Glitazones for type 2 diabetes
- Wound care
- Glycoprotein IIb/IIIa receptor inhibitor
- Implantable cardioverter defibrillators
- Autologous cartilage transplantation
- Riluzole for motor neuron disease
- Ritalin for hyperactivity
- Ribavarin/alpha-interferon for hepatitis C
- Cox II inhibitors for rheumatoid arthritis

international development of a shared understanding of the methodology underpinning the construction of high quality clinical guidelines. However, despite this academic and professional leadership, there has (until now) been no national authority for clinical guidelines in England and Wales. Moreover, although clinical guideline developers have been moving in the same direction, there remains a degree of variation in approaches to clinical guideline development.

The DoH and the National Assembly for Wales have charged NICE with developing and disseminating 'robust and authoritative' clinical guidelines. In constructing clinical guidelines, NICE is expected to take into account both clinical and cost effectiveness. Where relevant, NICE seeks to produce parallel clinical guidelines for patients and their carers.

In the past, many clinical guidelines have been produced by professional associations to aid the professional practice of their members. NICE is an SHA of the NHS, and its clinical guideline programmes will need to pay attention to the legitimate interest of all those with an involvement in the quality of NHS services.

Key principles

Ten key principles (Table 5) will underpin the way in which NICE handles clinical guideline developments on behalf of the NHS. There will be many differences among the different kinds of clinical guidelines produced by NICE, but the key principles should be relevant to the approach for all of them.

Table 5. Ten key principles for NHS clinical guidelines.

1	The objective of clinical guidelines is to improve the quality of clinical care by making available to health professionals and patients well-founded advice on best practice
2	Quality care is based on clinical effectiveness – the extent to which the health status of patients can be expected to be enhanced by clinical interventions
3	Quality of care in the NHS necessarily includes giving due attention to the cost effectiveness of healthcare interventions
4	NHS clinical guidelines are relevant to the care provided by the NHS throughout the NHS in England and Wales
5	NHS clinical guidelines are advisory
6	NHS clinical guidelines are based on the best possible research evidence, expert opinion and professional consensus
7	NHS clinical guidelines are developed using methods that command the respect of patients, the NHS and the NHS stakeholders
8	Although clinical guidelines are focused around the clinical care provided by clinicians, patients are to be treated as full and equal partners along with the relevant professional groups involved in a clinical guideline development
9	All those who might be affected by a clinical guideline deserve consideration within the clinical guideline development (usually including patients and their carers, service managers, the wider public, government and healthcare industries)
10	NHS clinical guidelines should be both ambitious and realistic in nature. They should set out the clinical care that might reasonably be expected throughout the NHS

Status of NHS clinical guidelines

NHS clinical guidelines will provide advice to assist decisions by practitioners and patients. They will be decision aids that will not have mandatory force, but the way the clinical guidelines have been developed and presented should be such that few recipients would have cause to dispute the basis of the recommendations.

Quality in clinical guidelines developments

There is general acceptance that all good clinical guidelines should have a number of features in common. These quality criteria were developed initially in the early 1990s in the USA, and have been developed further so that they can be applied routinely to any clinical guideline. The attributes include validity, reliability, reproducibility, clinical applicability and flexibility, clarity, multidisciplinary process, scheduled review and documentation. This approach seeks to ensure that biases inherent in clinical guideline production are minimised. Clinical guideline recommendations should be based on the best available evidence and, where this is not possible, demonstrate how expert judgement has been incorporated into the recommendations.

The Scottish Intercollegiate Guidelines Network's (SIGN) *Clinical guidelines: criteria for appraisal of clinical guidelines for national use,*[3] the more recent *Appraisal instrument for clinical guidelines,*[4] developed by the Healthcare Evaluation Unit at St George's Hospital Medical School, and the *Appraisal of guidelines for research and evaluation in Europe (AGREE)*[5] instrument presently under development, are all based on the above principles. NICE will also apply these principles when commissioning or developing its own clinical guidelines.

NICE's clinical guidelines will be seen as having a particularly authoritative position within the NHS. This has not necessarily been the case for those developed previously. For these reasons, the NHS and NICE will expect that clinical guideline development will have to give increased attention to patient interests and issues of cost effectiveness and implementation.

Responsibility for selecting the clinical guideline topics referred to NICE rests with the Secretary of State for Health and the National Assembly for Wales. The first programme is presented in Table 6 and was derived from a careful scrutiny of areas likely to have a significant impact on the NHS. The programme will be overseen by a Guidelines Committee chaired by Professor Martin Eccles.

Table 6. Clinical guidelines to complete or commission.

- Management of schizophrenia
- Prevention and treatment of pressure sores
- National cancer group programme
- Peptic ulcer and dyspepsia
- Depressive illness in the community
- Acute myocardial infarction
- Management of completed myocardial infarction in primary care
- Hypertension
- Multiple sclerosis
- Routine pre-operative investigations
- Non-insulin dependent diabetes

Referral advice

One of the key reasons for the establishment of NICE was to reduce variation in the quality of care provided by the NHS. Such variation of the quality of care can be manifested in many ways, including access from primary care into specialist centres. There is now considerable research describing the variability in general practitioner (GP) outpatient referral rates, but less understanding about the underlying reasons. Key to an effective and efficient health service is the appropriate and timely referral of those patients who will benefit from specialist intervention.

In October 1999, the DoH and the National Assembly for Wales invited NICE, in addition to its other programmes, to produce outpatient referral advice for GPs on when to refer patients to specialists (see Table 7). This was a challenging timetable in a field with little research evidence about how it should be approached.

Drawing on experience of developing local protocols in the South Thames region and Newcastle, a methodology was designed that adhered to NICE's generic principles of rigour, transparency and inclusion of all stakeholders. A steering group was convened to oversee the project. Advisory groups were created to modify and adapt draft advice created by the NICE project team. Each group consists of GPs, specialists and patient advocates. They are designed to provided advice on when patients should be referred; they are not clinical guidelines on how to manage patients. In the future, when NICE's guidelines programme is established, all its clinical guidelines will include 'referral advice'.

Table 7. Referral advice.

- Atopic eczema in children
- Acne
- Psoriasis
- Acute low back pain
- Osteoarthritis of the hip
- Osteoarthritis of the knee
- Glue ear in children
- Recurrent episodes of acute sore throat in children
- Dyspepsia
- Varicose veins
- Urinary tract (outflow) symptoms
- Menorrhagia

Clinical audit

NICE also has responsibility for supporting clinical audit. In addition to producing audit advice to accompany all its guidance, it has been allocated the budgets for the Royal College audit units, the national sentinel audits, and the confidential enquiries. It is in the process of reviewing these to assess how they can best support the drive towards clinical and cost effectiveness in the NHS.

Conclusion

What is the contribution of NICE to the debate on NHS quality? NICE is unashamedly about defining best practice, based on the best research evidence that can be found, together with a systematic approach to seeking professional and public opinion. It is hoped that this will lead to informed expectations, both of what the profession hopes to achieve and of what the public can expect. Much of the guidance that NICE will issue in the coming year will be of specific relevance to the older patient, and therefore should assist in the implementation of the NSF for older people.

References

1   Department of Health. *The new NHS: modern dependable.* Cm 3807. London: HMSO, 1997.

2   Department of Health. *A first class service: quality in the new NHS.* London: HMSO, 1998.

3   Scottish Intercollegiate Guidelines Network. *Criteria for appraisal for national use.* Edinburgh: SIGN, 1995.

4   Cluzeau F, Littlejohns P, Grimshaw J, Feder J, *et al.* Development and application of a generic methodology to assess the quality of clinical guidelines. *Int J Qual Healthcare* 1999; **11**: 21–8.

5   Littlejohns P, Cluzeau F. *Promoting the rigorous development of clinical guidelines in Europe through the creation of a common appraisal instrument.* Amsterdam: Scientific Basis For Health Services, 1997.

5 | Approaches to measuring the quality of healthcare

James Coles
Director, CASPE Research

Rather than attempt to address the whole subject of quality and the myriad of measurement and assessment methodologies and technologies, this chapter will consider only two aspects of the topic:

1 The need to retain a balance between the requirement to deliver accountability upward, and the likelihood that achieving and delivering continuing quality improvement requires motivation at a more local level.

2 The attributes required of quantitative information if it is to be useful in helping to achieve such improvements.

These two aspects will have a major impact on whether or not these technologies succeed in their overall aim of improving quality of care and, in so doing, draw out some issues of national and strategic focus, linking them to more clinically focused current experiences of data gathering, collation and interpretation.

Retaining a balance

The relationship between the demands from the Department of Health (DoH) at the centre and local initiatives can create a healthy tension for improving quality. The centre can challenge local managers and clinicians to make progress where previously inertia might have prevailed, while local clinicians challenge the centre to justify its demands for such monitoring information and bring about further refinements to this approach.

However, there is a need to ensure that we do not get fixated on the information itself, or in merely acquiring a library of standards, guidelines or benchmarks. This development of knowledge about good practice must be balanced by providing assistance to practitioners in operationalising and implementing improvements to deliver against such standards. Additionally, there needs to be a focus on moving the whole of the NHS forward, rather than concentrating on a few enthusiastic pilot sites.

These points were taken up in part in the DoH publication, *A first class service*,[1] when it stated:

> The drive to place quality at the heart of the NHS is not about ticking checklists – it is about changing thinking ... Driving up standards will rely on the commitment and expertise of all those who work in the health service.

As well as commitment and expertise, quality improvement requires a sharing of that expertise and a sense of partnership across the NHS – that is, between central bodies such as the DoH and the National Institute for Clinical Excellence, the Commission for Health Improvement (CHI) and the service itself – rather than the creation of an overtly confrontational relationship. Since the publication of *A first class service*[1] (and subsequent more detailed documents) there has been a greater sense of shared objectives, although there remains a certain mistrust of the centre's demands for monitoring information that is often seen (sometimes mistakenly) to be incomplete, inaccurate or inappropriate. Such negative views can lead to perverse behaviour locally, further distorting the

Table 1. The six domains of the high level indicators within the NHS Performance Assessment Framework.

	Indicators	
Domain	Type	No
Health improvement	Mortality	5
	Registrations	2
Fair access	Registrations	2
	Activity rates	2
	Waiting list	1
Effective delivery of appropriate healthcare	Activity +ve/–ve	5/1
	Efficient discharge	1
	Prescribing	1
Efficiency	Activity rates	1
	Length of stay	1
	Unit cost	2
	Prescribing	1
Patient/carer experience	Waiting times/list	3
	Failed appointments	2
	Delays	1
Health outcomes	Mortality	4
	Unplanned admissions	2
	Adverse events	1

information obtained and distracting attention from the overall objective of improved care.

Inevitably, the emphasis on high level monitoring at a national level will lead to information being collected that is different from that perceived to be 'ideal' locally. National level data remove much of the detail that might support local clinicians in reviewing and interpreting how to improve care on a day-to-day basis. Table 1 shows the six domains of the high level indicators within the NHS Performance Assessment Framework (PAF), with the distribution of indicators summarised by type of indicator. Many people would readily accept the six domains identified as important components of a quality service, but those working at the operational level may have more difficulty in accepting that activity, registration and other administrative data tell us much about quality. Even mortality indicators are likely to be seen as insufficiently sensitive or relevant.

Yet, according to the national press recently, in reference to the care of older people, 'the NHS is ageist'. This assertion was based on comments made in a recently published Age Concern Report[2] that:

▌ older people have reduced access to coronary care units, transplants and cancer treatment

▌ waiting times and delayed operations are used as rationing mechanisms

▌ older people experience rudeness and lack of dignity in treatment.

From this not very startling fact it might be deduced that gross strategic level information also has its place in addressing quality issues within the NHS.

In reply to Age Concern's report, the Minister, John Hutton, announced that the government is determined to provide older people with care that meets their needs and is fast, efficient and sensitive. This takes us neatly on from considering the PAF to the more clinically orientated National Service Frameworks (NSFs), especially the NSF currently being developed for the care of older people.

Most people involved in healthcare would probably say that they are more supportive of the concept of NSFs than of the high level indicators just described. They would be expected to be more closely concerned with operational standards of delivering high quality patient care rather than with strategic issues. It is pleasing to note that NSFs are based on information already published, that they are establishing clearly defined standards with supporting rationale, developing criteria to assess performance against these standards, and providing examples of good practice for achieving these criteria. However, there is still some way to go since, at the moment, many of the criteria are interim and heavily process based (eg evidence of plans being in existence, etc), which recognises the dearth of appropriate outcomes data. Also, while NSFs will be mandatory and monitored centrally, their real success in delivering better patient care will clearly remain at the local level and in the way in which they are used to motivate change.

Some of the factors (drawn from research findings) known to be necessary to stimulate and support change at a local level are:

- the need to gain agreement about local objectives and the need for change
- the need for professional consonance
- the recognition that information provides a stimulus, but does not prescribe the solution
- the need for a developmental and supportive environment
- the need to monitor information to reinforce the impact of changes to date.

These points emphasise the importance of an appropriate environment, a level of consensus about the need and direction of change, and information that motivates and reinforces progress. The publication of the NSFs and a centralist approach to monitoring will not necessarily be sufficient to deliver the improved quality as sought by their objectives – quality improvement requires participation by those directly involved in patient care.

Attributes required of quantitative information

The NSFs require information both to enable local managers and clinicians to identify areas for action and to monitor progress, and also to report upward to the DoH (the CHI or similar bodies). To achieve this, the quantitative information will need to be appropriate and robust.

Judging from experience to date, it seems likely that one of the sources from which the early NSFs will draw will be the work done by CASPE, the Royal Colleges, and the Unit for Healthcare Epidemiology at the University of Oxford in developing health outcome indicators for the National Centre for Health Outcomes Development. Ten reports focused on individual clinical conditions (see Table 2).

Rationale and methodology underpinning the outcomes development work

A similar methodology was followed for each of the 10 conditions looked at. Each of the multiprofessional working groups was asked to identify a comprehensive list of known effective interventions relevant to the particular condition. This was assisted, but not constrained, by the use of a health outcome model (Fig 1).

This approach follows the causal pathway from the population level through to secondary and tertiary care. The model is really only a framework, and in any particular case may not represent an exhaustive list of outcomes or interventions. However, it has proved useful as a stimulus, assisting and prompting the working groups to identify the important interventions and to develop ideas about desirable objectives and outcome measures at each stage through the pathway.

Having identified the interventions, the next stage was to specify the goals of each intervention, which were then grouped by type, such as reduction or avoidance of risk, improving functioning or support of carers – of particular relevance when considering older people.

Table 2. List of conditions for which NCHOD has produced outcome indicators.

Asthma	Myocardial infarction
Breast cancer	Normal pregnancy and childbirth
Cataract	Severe mental illness
Diabetes Mellitus	Stroke
Fractured proximal femur	Urinary incontinence

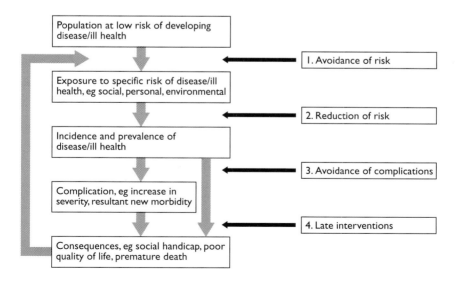

Fig 1. *Health outcome model for deriving health outcome indicators.*

A further factor that needed to be recognised was the varying perspectives and emphases of the condition that could be taken by particular stakeholders in healthcare. For example, a patient may be less interested in specific clinical measurements or assessments, and more interested in a return of functional abilities or in his or her psychological well-being. However, the population as a whole (both as taxpayers and as potential patients) has a valid perspective in seeking to establish what a particular intervention can be expected to achieve for the population as a whole, rather than in an individual case. These multiple perspectives were also considered by the working groups; the indicators, as they were identified, were mapped on to a matrix such as the one shown for stroke in Table 3.[3]

This aide served the purpose of identifying any possible gaps in the range of indicators identified. It was considered that each row and column should contain some indicators, in order to address each health outcome goal that had been established and to ensure coverage of each measurement perspective, but that it was not appropriate to force an indicator into each cell across the matrix.

As well as trying to ensure that the indicators identified were fit for purpose (ie were relevant), had a 'product champion' within the working group and, where possible, strong evidence to support their inclusion, there was also concern to ensure that they should be collected accurately and robustly. A great deal of time and effort was therefore taken to define each indicator as fully as possible. The elements of the specification are shown in Table 4 and included in each of the 10 reports.

Table 3. Matrix for determining health outcome indicators for stroke.[3]

Health outcomes goal	Primary measurement perspective		
	Population	Professional	Patient/carer
Reduce/avoid risk of first stroke or subsequent stroke	eg BP level in GP population		
Reduce deaths from stroke		eg 30 day case fatality	
Reduce or avoid complications from stroke		Avoidance of pressure sores	
Improve function and well-being after stroke			eg Barthel Index
Support carers			eg Carer burden

BP = blood pressure; GP = general practitioner.

Table 4. Required specification of health outcome indicators.

Specification heading:

- Indicator title
- Characteristics:
  - perspective
  - specificity
  - measurement attributes
- Aim of intervention
- Indicator definition
- Rationale
- Potential uses
- Potential users
- Possible confounding variables
- Data sources
- Data quality
- Comments
- Conclusions and further work required

It was clear that not all indicators could be supported by current data collection systems, but the definitions are complete and permit indicator development where local circumstances make this possible, for example, through record linkage or enhanced information technology systems either at present or when future developments come on stream.

Summary

In conclusion, this chapter has looked at two separate aspects of quality assessment: first, the importance of understanding the environment in which such assessments take place; secondly, the need for information to be collected in a robust and consistent form if appropriate assessment, either at local level or at the centre, is to be valuable. These two themes come together within a single principle. For progress to be made in quality improvement (and the assessment thereof) throughout the NHS, it is necessary for such initiatives to gain and build on local respect and support – the trick is knowing how to obtain that support.

As suggested earlier, researchers have found some factors that are necessary to motivate change. These include shared objectives and shared perceptions of the relevance of specific activities, together with specific approaches to data collection (while recognising that others may have different but just as valid requirements).

The NSFs seem to be a positive way of moving towards such a shared understanding – but they are still in the early stages of development. Care must be taken to nurture and foster such partnerships rather than, through a lack of understanding or appreciation, stalling them at the outset.

References

1   Department of Health. *A first class service: quality in the new NHS.* London: HMSO, 1998.

2   Age Concern. *Turning your back on us: older people and the NHS.* London: Age Concern, 1999.

3   Rudd A, Goldacre M, Amess M, Fletcher J, *et al* (eds). *Health outcome indicators: stroke. Report of a working group to the Department of Health.* Oxford: National Centre for Health Outcomes Development, 1999.

SECTION 3

Quality of care studies

6 | Using existing information databases to measure outcomes in fractured proximal femur

Alastair Mason

Consultant Epidemiologist, National Centre for Health Outcomes Development

Health outcome indicators

The Department of Health started to take health outcome indicators seriously in 1993 with the setting up the Central Health Outcomes Unit (CHOU). Two other important events happened that year. First, the Faculty of Public Health Medicine completed a feasibility study of health outcome indicators;[1] secondly, the University of Surrey published the first set of comparative outcome indicators.[2] It soon became apparent from these that information based solely on existing data would not be adequate, and a project was commissioned to develop ideal outcome indicators for 10 conditions.

In 1998, CHOU was outsourced as the National Centre for Health Outcomes Development with two sites:

 ▌ the Unit of Healthcare Epidemiology, Oxford University, responsible for developing new indicators, and

 ▌ the London School of Hygiene and Tropical Medicine, responsible for the production and publication of national comparative health statistics.

After a considerable gestation period, the reports of 10 working groups developing ideal outcome indicators were published in September 1999. In these reports, health outcomes were defined as changes in health, health status or risk factors affecting health that may be the result of disease or of the effect of the interventions to prevent or treat it. Indicators were considered as providing pointers to circumstances that may be worth further investigation. Ideal indicators were defined as being statistical measures of what should – and realistically could – be known about a condition.

The approach to health indicators adopted by the working groups was based on four concepts:

1 They aimed to be health, not health service, orientated.

2 Unlike previously, there was no constraint to develop indicators solely based on existing data.

3 A comprehensive approach was adopted, based on an outcome model.

4 A multipurpose set of indicators was chosen. It was multi-user because it provided a menu from which users could choose indicators to meet their own requirements.

Fractured proximal femur

One of the 10 conditions addressed was fractured proximal femur, which is a common concern for older people. Two types of indicator were developed: indicators that can be obtained from routine data systems and those that need special surveys. Recommendations were made about the implementation status of the indicators, listing those that could be implemented immediately, and others which needed further work before they could be recommended for implementation.

Two indicators recommended as needing further work were, first, the admission rate for second contralateral fractured femur and, secondly, the rate of ipsilateral hip surgery within 120 days of a previous procedure. Although the Office of Population, Censuses and Surveys (OPCS-4)[3] procedure coding provides a distinction between the right and the left hip operated upon, current completion rates of these data fields is poor. Indicators on this subject will not be available until the coding of this information has been improved.

Two *proxy* outcome indicators were also considered to need further work:

1 The rate of accident and emergency attendances for distal radius fracture was suggested as a proxy measure for falls. At present, there is no good evidence supporting this supposition.

2 The working group also considered measuring the rate of use of thromboprophylactics. A commissioned literature review showed that the evidence of the effectiveness of the intervention was not good enough to justify using the thromboprophylaxis rate as an outcome indicator.

Measures for fractured proximal femur in which an NHS trust should be particularly interested are shown in Table 1.

Case fatality rates (CFRs) and readmission rates are worth comparing between trusts. Piloting studies in stroke care have shown that comparative pressure sore rates are difficult to interpret, and that pressure sores should be reported as sentinel events with all occurrences investigated.[4]

Table 1. Outcome indicators for fractured femur relevant at trust level.

Routine:

- comparative case fatality rate
- comparative re-admission rate
- occurrence of pressure sores

Periodic survey:

- patient focused measures at 120 days
- measure of postoperative pain

A trust should also periodically carry out surveys of the occurrence of postoperative pain and of patient focused measures, such as attainment of patient specified goals, return to former activity, daily living scores and mobility levels, collected 120 days after the event.[5]

Piloting femur outcome indicators

The two outcome indicators for which piloting information is presented in this chapter are CFR and the percentage of patients whose pre-operative stay was two or more days. Table 2 shows the major components of the pilot study that used one of the best available sets of hospital episode data, the Oxford Record Linkage Study (ORLS). Our investigation obtained data on 17,684 admissions between 1979 and 1993 with a diagnosis of fractured neck of femur. The 10 hospitals reviewed accounted for 91% of the cases.

The measurement of CFRs had been recommended by the working group as a direct measure of health outcome useful for hospital comparisons, but the group was undecided whether it should be

Table 2. Outcome indicators for fractured femur derived from the Oxford Record Linkage Study.

Case fatality rate:

- effect of different time periods
- effect of age and sex

Proportion with pre-operative stay >2 days:

- effect of age or sex
- comparison with case fatality rate

calculated at 30 days or 120 days (the latter being the current European standard). The drawback of this indicator is that its calculation requires the accurate linking of activity and mortality data.

Fig 1 shows the age/sex effect on CFRs measured at 120 days. Both sexes exhibit an extremely marked increase in CFR with age. Figures 2 and 3 show comparisons between the 10 hospitals in the ORLS using the 30 and 120 day CFRs. Hospitals 2 and 7 have rates for both indicators that need closer investigation. Table 3 shows how the rankings of the hospitals compare when the CFR is measured at 30, 120 and 365 days and during the

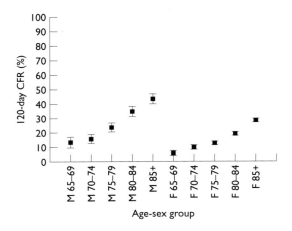

Fig 1. *Case fatality rate (CFR): age/sex effect using 120-day CFR* (M = men; F = women).

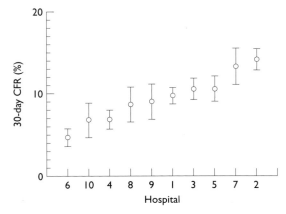

Fig 2. *30-day case fatality rate from 10 hospitals in the Oxford Record Linkage Study.*

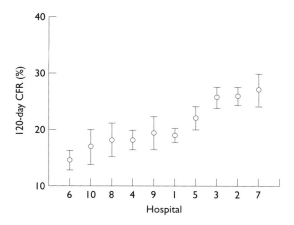

Fig 3. *120-day case fatality rate from 10 hospitals in the Oxford Record Linkage Study.*

Table 3. Comparison of hospital rankings measuring the case fatality rate at 30, 120 and 365 days and during the in-hospital admission.

Hospital no.	Case fatality rate (days)							
	30		120		365		In-hospital	
	Rank	%	Rank	%	Rank	%	Rank	%
6	1	4.7	1	14.5	1	23.9	1	5.4
10	2	6.8	2	16.9	2	25.4	6	11.0
4	2	6.8	3	18.1	5	29.4	2	9.2
8	4	8.7	3	18.1	3	27.7	5	10.2
9	5	9.0	6	19.4	7	30.6	7	11.1
1	6	9.7	5	18.9	4	29.1	3	9.4
5	7	10.6	7	22.0	6	30.5	8	11.6
3	7	10.6	8	25.7	9	35.9	3	9.4
7	9	13.3	10	27.0	10	36.3	9	12.3
2	10	14.2	9	25.9	8	35.8	10	15.6

in-hospital admission. There is a close correlation between the 30 and 120 days' rankings, but they both correlate poorly with the in-hospital rate. From this study, it would not seem to matter too much for interhospital comparisons whether the preferred indicator was CFR at 30 or 120 days.

The major effect of age and sex has already been noted. Tables 4 and 5 show the CFR hospital rankings at 30 and 120 days, respectively, compared according to an age standardised mortality rate calculated for the same periods. There is a close correlation for both time periods between the CFR and the standardised rate. It would seem that the hospitals reviewed had similar patients of a similar age-sex mix.

Thus, the CFR can be used for hospital comparisons, but any interpretation of the information needs to take into account the marked effect of age. If there is an outlier, the first question to ask is whether the age and sex mix in that unit is in any way different from other hospitals.

Delays to operation

The other indicator that was piloted was an indirect proxy measure relating to delay before operation. It can be easily obtained from routine data collected on a patient administration system. Because it is an easy indicator to calculate, and the requisite data are already collected, it has been proposed by many authorities as a potential health outcome indicator. A literature search commissioned by the working group in fact showed no firmly proven link between the length of pre-operative stay and resulting outcomes.[5] Shorter pre-operative stays do not necessarily lead to fewer deaths.

Table 4. The case fatality rate (CFR) hospital rankings at 30 days.

| Hospital | CFR rank | Standardised mortality ratio | | |
		Rank	Ratio	CI
6	1	1	46	(36–57)
4	2	2	67	(55–78)
10	2	3	68	(46–890)
8	4	4	81	(60–1,020)
9	5	5	87	(65–109)
1	6	6	93	(83–103)
3	7	7	102	(89–115)
5	7	9	105	(89–121)
7	9	9	130	(107–153)
2	10	10	135	(122–148)

CI = confidence interval.

Table 5. Case fatality rate (CFR) hospital rankings at 120 days.

Hospital	CFR rank	Standardised mortality ratio		
		Rank	Ratio	CI
6	1	1	67	(59–76)
10	2	2	79	(64–95)
8	3	3	80	(66–95)
4	3	4	84	(75–93)
1	5	5	86	(79–92)
9	6	6	89	(74–104)
5	7	7	104	(93–114)
3	8	8	118	(108–128)
2	9	9	117	(109–126)
7	10	10	125	(109–141)

CI = confidence interval.

Figure 4, a comparison of the 10 hospitals for this indicator, reveals three hospitals that appear to be performing worse than the rest. At first sight, this seems to be a case for instant intervention from a regional office or even the Commission for Health Improvement. However, when the hospital rankings for the pre-operative delay indicator are compared with those for CFRs at 30, 120 and 365 days, there is a different picture.

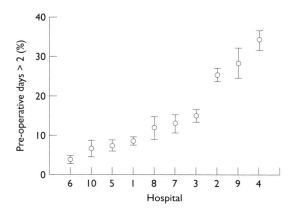

Fig 4. *Ten hospitals ranked by percentage pre-operative days greater than two for fractured femur.*

Hospital 9 is ranked 9 in terms of pre-operative delay, but is respectably in the middle in terms of CFRs, while hospital 4, bottom in terms of pre-operative delay, is among the top three for CFRs.

This study confirms the working group's view that delay before operation should not be used as a proxy health outcome indicator for comparing the ability of hospitals to treat patients with fractured femur, despite the ease with which it can be calculated.

Conclusion

Health outcome indicators are being developed which will make possible sensible comparison of hospital performance, and thus identify places that might have problems. However, in using indicators it is essential to bear in mind the following 'health warnings':

▍ indicators should be used with care, and only for the purposes for which they have been designed

▍ indicators only *indicate* areas worth investigating further

▍ credible indicators require high quality data that is linked. This will be available only when there is a proper investment in information production facilities.

References

1   McColl A, Gulliford M. *Population health outcome indicators for the NHS: a feasibility study.* London: Faculty of Public Health Medicine, 1993.
2   Department of Health. *Population health indicators for the NHS: a consultation document.* London: Department of Health, 1993.
3   Office of Population Censuses and Surveys. *Tabular list of the classification of surgical operations and procedures* (4th revision). London: HMSO, 1990.
4   Rudd A, Pearson MG, Georgiou A (eds). *Measuring clinical outcome in stroke (acute care).* London: Royal College of Physicians, 2000.
5   Fairbank J, Goldacre M, Mason A, Wilkinson E, *et al* (eds). *Fractured proximal femur. Report of a working group to the Department of Health.* Oxford: National Centre for Health Outcomes Development, 1999.

7 | The national sentinel audit for stroke and its lessons for clinical governance

Anthony Rudd

Associate Director, Clinical Effectiveness and Evaluation Unit,
Royal College of Physicians

This chapter will focus on the results of the national sentinel audit for stroke (NSAS),[1] how the audit was developed and what the impact has been. It will address issues of data quality and questions that arise from that. The problems of measuring the quality of stroke care using true outcome measures will also be discussed.

Background

Stroke is a difficult disease to audit, but not necessarily any more difficult than many of the other areas included in the National Service Framework for older people. Studying disease in older people is an intrinsically complex process, which is why it needs to be done by some of the best physicians in the country. Stroke is not a single disease, but rather a clinical syndrome caused by a range of pathologies. It has an unpredictable natural history, even if variable pathology is taken into account. It is largely a disease of older people (but not exclusively, as it also occurs in children and young adults), with half the strokes in the UK occurring in people over the age of 75 years. When considering this age group, normal ageing processes have to be considered as these will affect the natural history of the disease. The patients suffering from stroke come from a wide range of social backgrounds and circumstances which will also affect the outcome. This will be particularly relevant if the outcome used is the proportion of people discharged to their own homes or if measures of quality of life are used. Finally, measurement of outcome after stroke is hindered by the lack of evidence linking process with outcome. Table 1 shows some of the areas where the lack of evidence is a particular problem.

It is widely accepted that checking the safety of the swallowing reflex is important, but there is actually little evidence to show that stopping

Table 1. Aspects of stroke medicine with limited evidence base to determine best practice.

* Acute therapies
* Many areas of rehabilitation
* Patient and carer satisfaction
* Prevention of complications (eg aspiration pneumonia, spasticity, depression)
* Handicap reducing measures

somebody who is aspirating from eating or drinking will prevent them developing pneumonia. Paucity of evidence linking process with outcome is particularly evident for measures aimed at reducing handicap.

The World Health Organization (WHO) set targets internationally in the Helsingborg declaration in 1995.[2] Some of the key targets are outcome measures, while others are descriptions of the way in which care for stroke victims should be provided (Table 2). One of the measures included is the incidence of stroke recurrence in patients surviving two years after stroke. WHO states that this should be reduced below 20%, and death due to vascular disease to below 40% by 2005. This target has been set without, as far as I am aware, any evidence to show that it is achievable. Many of the process measures proposed, however, received the overwhelming support of the stroke profession.

The national sentinel audit for stroke

The NSAS covered England, Wales and Northern Ireland. Scotland has recently also conducted an audit of stroke services. As a result, there is a

Table 2. Helsingborg declaration: key targets for stroke care.[2]

* Incidence of stroke recurrence in patients surviving two years reduced below 20%
* Death due to vascular diseases below 40%
* All patients should have access to:
  - secondary prevention
  - specialist stroke team or stroke unit
  - rehabilitation services as soon as medical condition permits
* Rehabilitation should be provided by an interdisciplinary team trained in stroke management
* All states should have a system for evaluation for stroke management and quality assessment

clearer picture of the overall quality of stroke care in the UK than anywhere else in Europe. The NSAS was set up to look at the way that each service is organised and at the process of care for individual patients.

The organisational audit covered a wide range of domains, including:

▌ the numbers of patients being looked after

▌ the co-ordination and documentation of care

▌ the training of the staff, and

▌ access to information.

The process audit involved the detailed examination of up to 40 sets of notes from consecutive patients admitted over a three-month period at the beginning of 1998. This is the first time there has been an audit of this size that has attempted to look not only at the medical care of patients, but also at the work of all the relevant disciplines from the time of admission to six months after the stroke. Thus, not only did the audit cross disciplines but also sectors – involving primary and secondary healthcare as well as social service support. Table 3 gives the domains audited.

This was a broad-ranging audit; it might be argued that it was over-ambitious. The audit tool was developed over a period of two years by the Intercollegiate Stroke Working Party, a group of professionals originally set up by the late Anthony Hopkins. The working party included representatives from all the professional associations and colleges that have a role or an interest in the management of stroke patients. For a disease like stroke where the evidence base is not as strong as it might be, it was important to have professionals deciding what the audit standards

Table 3. National sentinel audit for stroke: domains audited.

Organisational audit	Process audit
• Interdisciplinary services	• Initial assessment
• Staff knowledge and skills	• Clinical assessment
• Teamworking records	• Functional assessment
• Team meetings	• Multidisciplinary involvement
• Agreed assessment measures	• Management planning
• Availability of information	• Continence management
• Clinical audit	• Secondary prevention
• Communication with patients and carers	• Information provision

would be, so that those standards would carry the weight of the professions. One of the roles of all individuals in the working party was to consult with their professional societies at every stage in the process of the development of the tool.

The tool was subjected to a Delphi exercise, ie using a large number of clinicians from each of the professions to try to identify the key areas that were thought important to audit. This was followed by a piloting exercise which included an inter-rater reliability study involving teaching hospitals, district general hospitals and community hospitals. On the basis of this process, the Clinical Effectiveness and Evaluation Unit of the Royal College of Physicians developed 'help booklets', which were detailed explanations about how each of the questions should be answered and where there were potential difficulties. These booklets have demonstrated the importance of going through a pilot exercise to identify the difficulties. When the inter-rater reliability study was repeated in the main study there were considerable improvements.

Results of the audit

A total of 206 hospitals participated in the audit (80% of the trusts within England, Wales and Northern Ireland which treat acute stroke patients). Nearly 7,000 sets of notes were audited, representing almost 50% of all admissions for stroke in the participating trusts during the three-month study period.

The organisational audit showed that about 50% of the trusts have a specialist stroke team, 64% have a consultant with responsibility for stroke, and the vast majority have access to the basic therapies (physiotherapy, occupational and speech therapy). Many would argue that clinical psychology should be an intrinsic part of the stroke team, but access to it is limited.

The process audit showed that in many areas there were poor levels of compliance with the standards that had been set. For example, the standard for assessment of swallowing, which is to have assessed swallowing at least once during the hospital admission, was achieved in only just over half the cases. There was some evidence that cognitive function was assessed in about 20% of patients. One of the key investigations that medical students learn to do when people come into hospital with a stroke is to check for a visual field defect, yet over half the patient notes showed no record of visual field. One of the standards set for nutritional assessment is that the patient has been weighed at least once during the course of their admission, but less than half the notes audited had a weight recorded.

The standard of secondary prevention was little better. Only 88% of patients with cerebral infarction received either antithrombotic or anticoagulant medication. There was poor documentation of disability and handicap. Standards were significantly better for patients who had been on stroke units compared with general rehabilitation units, but the latter were better than general medical wards. This perhaps explains why stroke units have better outcomes than alternative forms of care. However, only 18% of all the patients in the audit spent more than half their time in hospital on a stroke unit.

What was the audit actually measuring?

Was the audit an acceptable tool to use and an acceptable process to go through? Although participation in the audit was voluntary, 80% of trusts took part (some perhaps more enthusiastically than others). There were many positive comments about the audit, with many people saying that, for the first time, this was an audit they found useful and which could be used to argue with the trust managers for more resources. The second cycle of the audit had nearly as many trusts participating (72%) as the first cycle, despite the audit being repeated only a year later.

Methodological considerations

Is the audit valid?

It is difficult to be certain about the validity of the audit, but there are a few pointers which suggest that the results reflect what is happening in reality. First, those units which, through personal knowledge, would be expected to be offering a good service performed better than those trusts which were relatively anonymous within the stroke world. That stroke units show better quality care would be expected. Individual trust results were returned to them within three months of submitting the data, their results having been compared with the national mean. There were only a few queries about the data. If the results had not tallied with what people believed was going on within their own trusts, we would have been the first to hear about it. Seventeen regional workshops were set up in June and July 1999, bringing together the participating trusts and the leaders from those trusts to discuss their results and to present the regional variations. This was a further opportunity for people to question the data.

Clearly, however, the data have flaws. The first problem is that only hospitalised patients were audited. The rate of non-hospitalisation for stroke varies from 20% in South London to 50% in the original Oxford

Community register data,[3] so a significant proportion of stroke patients were not audited. Secondly, even within hospitalised patients it is not possible to be sure that the notes really were a consecutive series representative of what goes on within a hospital at all times.

The major problem concerns the retrieval of notes. Anyone who has been involved in audit will be aware of how difficult it is to get notes out of hospital records' departments. In some trusts it is difficult to get the notes of dead patients; in other hospitals, it is difficult to get the notes of people who are still actively under follow-up in outpatients. If the auditors were unable to retrieve the notes of a patient, they were allowed to select the next patient; this may have either artificially inflated or reduced the mortality rates.

Inter-rater reliability

Inter-rater reliability is of major importance when many auditors from a wide variety of professional backgrounds are completing the forms. Table 4 gives the scores for inter-rater reliability using Kappa to provide an index of the level of agreement between raters across a selection of the variables. The kappa values range from 0.55 and 0.87. A value of 1 indicates perfect agreement while 0 indicates that similarity was due to chance. The figures in this study represent a high degree of reliability for such audits. Inter-rater reliability is not therefore a major issue in terms of interpreting the data. As far as we are aware, no previous audits have reported such high values.

Many different people audited these notes, each of whom will have a different agenda. It may well be that a hospital physician or stroke physician will be particularly keen on getting a particular sort of result from the audit. This is not to suggest that it is done in any way

Table 4. Range of Kappa scores for inter-rater reliability in a selection of variables from the national sentinel audit for stroke.

Assessment	Kappa value
Acute assessment on admission	0.55–0.73
Assessment during admission	0.64–0.8
Multidisciplinary involvement	0.59–0.76
Secondary prevention	0.6–0.8
Discharge planning	0.76–0.87
Follow-up and review	0.81–0.86

deliberately, but if they have at the back of their mind that their service is awful and more resources are needed, obviously it is in their interests to come out with poor results. On the other hand, if the physician has just been provided with extra resource, but has been off playing golf instead of developing the service, maybe the results will appear slightly better. The audit official within the department or the audit co-ordinator will perhaps do a better job, but it may be much more difficult for them; if they have a pile of audits to do in a limited time, their attention to detail may not be as great. Alternatively, they may have more time than the clinician and produce more reliable results. These questions are particularly important in the context of an audit which involves looking not just at the hospital notes but also at the notes from all the therapists and social workers.

A big problem for this sort of audit is that it is recorded retro-spectively. It is recording what was written down, not necessarily what was actually done to the patient. A prospective audit was considered, but it was dismissed as being far too complex in terms of the time and cost involved.

The issue of reliability of the results for an audit, ostensibly a national audit but in which 20% of trusts did not participate, also needs to be considered. Figure 1 shows the Z-scores for the organisational audit versus the process audit. These data could be used to identify the trusts with a particularly poor service in need of remedial action – particularly important with the development of clinical governance. Those at the lower end of the charts know that others are achieving better; they know there is room for improvement, and that in order to catch up with their peers they should look both at their organisation of care and at their staff expertise.

What about the other 20% of hospitals that did not participate? The suspicion is that they possibly contain some of the weaker trusts in the country, so the poorly performing participating trusts may actually not be in the lowest percentiles. If audit of this sort is to be done with clinical governance as one of the objectives, one of the questions that needs to be raised is whether or not it should be compulsory.

Feasibility

There is no doubt that audit of this type is difficult and time consuming. Although I was involved in designing the forms, it still took me 20–30 minutes to complete a form for each patient, not including the time spent retrieving the notes. Others reported spending as much as an hour per patient. It was often difficult to get the data from multiple data

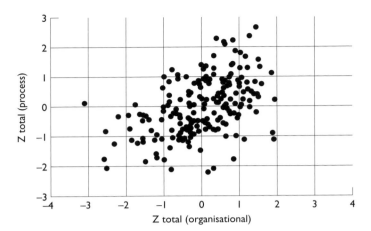

Fig 1. *Organisational and process audit totals by region.* The overall organisational audit score (max range 0–100) was standardised into a Z total with mean zero and standard deviation 1. The organisational Z total of a trust was then plotted against its process Z total in the scatterplots. A few trusts did not have both scores. Trusts with above average scores in both organisational and process audits appear in the top right-hand quadrant, and those with below average for both sections in the lower left-hand quadrant. Trusts in the two other quadrants performed above average on one section of the audit but not on the other (correlation coefficient 0.47, $p < 0.001$).

sources. It was considerably easier for those patients in my trust who were managed on the stroke unit where there is a unified set of notes, but it was difficult for those not admitted to the stroke unit. All the data had to be taken from the notes – no data were easily obtainable by simply downloading from the hospital administration system.

The cost of the whole audit at central level was approximately £200,000 for the two cycles. This cost does not include the time of everybody who participated at a local level. Audit cannot be done without a considerable financial resource.

Are there alternative methods?

It is possible to extract the two or three key questions which could be used to identify the underperforming trusts from the data we have. Visual field assessments and the recording of the presence or absence of neglect will pick up the majority of those severely underperforming trusts. If the sole purpose of the audit is to identify for the Commission for Health Improvement (CHI) those trusts that need to be visited, it can probably be done quite easily with a few simple questions. If the purpose is for trusts locally to be able to inform themselves about the quality of their service and how they compare with others, an audit of the sort we performed is probably needed.

Outcome measurement

Some more conventional measures of case mix rather than outcome were also selected in the stroke audit proforma. These data can be used to illustrate the variation between trusts and regions that needs explanation. One example is mortality rates, which vary considerably in different parts of the country.[1] It would appear that the best chance of surviving a stroke is in Northern Ireland. If you want to get out of hospital quickly go to Wessex, and do not go to Northern Ireland. If you want to be discharged with a Barthel score of 20 – in other words (at a crude level anyway) fully able – you will do much better in Trent than in South Thames. If you want to end up in a nursing home, go to the North West and not to North Thames. A huge proportion of people being discharged from hospitals in the North West go into residential or nursing home care compared with North Thames (27% vs 10%).

Davenport *et al* looked at the effects of case mix adjustment within a hospital service before and after the introduction of a stroke unit.[4] One group of patients was audited before the introduction of a stroke unit and another group after its development. If mortality is considered at 30 days and 12 months, dependence at 12 months, and whether or not patients were living at home, the introduction of a stroke unit was shown to have a beneficial effect on all the outcomes if uncorrected data and data corrected for age and sex were used. However, correcting for a more complex set of case mix adjustors showed no statistically significant effects on outcome before and after the introduction of the stroke unit. It is easy to misinterpret outcome data if sufficient care is not given to their interpretation. As yet, there is no universally accepted way of adjusting for case mix in stroke.

A study by Wolfe and colleagues looked at differences in outcome after stroke in centres around Europe[5,6] to see whether or not the way care was provided, and the huge variation in the way stroke is managed, around Europe have any impact on outcome. Table 5 shows mortality at three months, adjusted for case mix. The UK centres had significantly higher mortality than most of the other European centres, with Dijon in France performing best. Unfortunately, on outcomes in terms of the Barthel score at three months and the proportion of people discharged with a Barthel of 20 (little or no disability) the UK centres also did less well. We

Table 5. The European BIOMED Study of Stroke Care Group. Predicted 3-month mortality and functional ability (Barthel) for the entire data set using a model relating case mix and resource use to outcome for each centre. (Reprinted, with permission, from Ref 6.)

Country	Dead		Barthel <20		Barthel = 20	
	%	95% CI	%	95% CI	%	95% CI
UK 1	34	(25–42)	47	(38–56)	19	(14–24)
UK 2	31	(23–40)	48	(35–60)	21	(11–31)
UK 3	33	(28–38)	42	(32–52)	25	(15–34)
UK 4	38	(32–44)	29	(23–36)	33	(26–40)
UK 5	42	(35–49)	23	(17–29)	35	(28–43)
France	19	(14–24)	33	(25–40)	48	(42–54)
Portugal	36	(24–47)	40	(27–52)	24	(19–30)
Hungary	31	(19–42)	27	(15–40)	42	(33–51)
Spain	27	(23–32)	46	(40–52)	26	(22–31)
Germany 1	30	(26–33)	33	(29–38)	37	(33–40)
Germany 2	21	(15–27)	42	(34–51)	37	(29–44)
Italy	30	(26–33)	43	(38–47)	28	(25–31)

CI = confidence interval.

therefore not only have higher mortality rates, but our patients also end up more disabled.

There may be many explanations for this observation, other than the obvious one that the UK has a less effective health service. The data have been adjusted for most of the accepted case mix variables, but there was no adjustment for socio-economic variables. The culture of the patients may be important or there may be differences, as yet unrecognised, in premorbid risk factors, genetics or stroke pathology. The important point from the perspective of outcome measurement is that there is little to be gained from measuring these data if we have no idea what can be done to change our service to the sort of service provided in Dijon. Do I need to persuade my patients to eat more mustard or drink more red wine? Should we give our patients less rehabilitation because less is provided in Dijon? We do not know the answers – which raises the question about what to do with the outcome data if we measure it.

One possible alternative way of looking at outcomes would be if much more sensitive patient recovery curves could be developed for individual patients. Work in this area is being performed by Kate Tilling, a

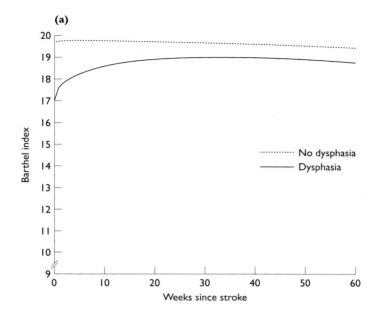

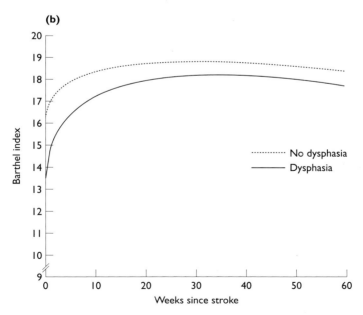

Fig 2. *Patterns of recovery after stroke according to patient characteristics whose effect varies over time in a patient aged below 80 with and without dysphasia* **(a)** *with no limb deficit;* **(b)** *with limb deficit.*

statistician at King's College London, who is plotting the recovery curves of Barthel scores for patients with differing baseline characteristics. Figure 2 illustrates some examples of these curves, showing how they vary according to age, presence or absence of dysphasia and limb weakness. This work is at an early stage of development, but individual recovery curves would be a powerful tool, both for the clinician on the ward – who would be able to identify when the patient is slipping off the recovery curve and something is going wrong – and also for audit and research.

Conclusion

This chapter has tried to show that, using an audit tool which is mainly measuring process, data can be collected that appear to be useful to the clinician and are probably much more informative than true outcome measures. If this can be achieved for a complex disease such as stroke, there is no reason why it could not be done for other diseases in older people. If this is to be done routinely, either current resources for audit need to be focused on to properly conducted national efforts rather than local studies, or data systems need to be developed so that information can be collected routinely from electronic patient records.

However, many questions remain to be resolved.

1 Should audit remain optional and anonymous, in the way that it has been done this time, or should it be taken over by the CHI? Audit should be compulsory if it is done for the purposes of clinical governance, and probably ought to be performed by independent auditors rather than by clinicians involved in the management of their patients.

2 How can care given be measured, not just recorded?

3 How can quality of care of all patients be measured, not just those admitted to hospital?

4 If outcome is measured, how will those outcomes be used constructively rather than just for the purposes of compiling crude league tables?

References

1 Rudd AG, Irwin P, Rutledge Z, Lowe D, *et al.* The national sentinel audit for stroke: a tool for raising standards of care. *J R Coll Physicians Lond* 1999; **33**: 460–4.

2 Adams HP. The importance of the Helsingborg declaration on stroke management in Europe. *J Intern Med* 1996; **240**: 169–71.

3 Oxfordshire Community Stroke Project. Incidence of stroke in Oxfordshire: first year's experience of a community stroke register. *Br Med J* 1983; **287**: 713–7.

Commentary: Why stop at antidepressants?

Simon Hatcher

Department of
Psychological
Medicine,
University of
Auckland, PB92019,
Auckland 1,
New Zealand

Simon Hatcher
*senior lecturer in
psychiatry*

s.hatcher@
auckland.ac.nz

Two problems arise when assessing treatments for depression. The first is specific to depression and the second is inherent in using randomised controlled trials as the sole evidence for deciding questions about treatment. Moncrieff and Kirsch focus on drug treatments, yet most of these issues also apply to non-drug interventions.[1]

Parker has described the problems of a "one size fits all" approach to trials of treatment for depression in which people with different severities of illness and symptoms are all included under the same heading of depression.[2] Ensuring participants remain blind to treatment is also a problem. Outcomes in depression trials are usually assessed with a rating scale. However, all rating scales are ordinal—someone who scores 20 on the Hamilton rating scale for depression is more depressed than someone who scores 10, but we can't say they are twice as depressed. Nevertheless, most researchers have assumed that you can, making the results (such as changes in mean scores) hard to interpret. Lastly, most trials of depression are for short periods. In the National Institute for Health and Clinical Excellence guidelines eight weeks is the cut-off for dividing trials into short term and long term studies.

Relying on randomised controlled trials as the sole evidence for making decisions about treatment also

One problem that psychological treatments don't share with drug treatments is the commercial considerations driving pharmacological research. This may affect the study design[3] and result in important publication bias because only positive findings are reported.[4]

Better evidence

So what is the way forward? Consumers need to participate in the design of treatment trials. They may be particularly helpful in devising better ways of engaging potential participants and in assessing outcome. Researchers need to think beyond conventional randomised controlled trials and consider patient preference trials or modified Zelen methods that combine the advantages of randomisation and observational studies.[5] Studies on treatment in depression need to be longer than a few weeks and they should report recruitment rates. Lastly registration of all new treatment trials and full disclosure of results needs to happen.

In the meantime, however, patients, clinicians, and funders still have to make decisions about treatment. These decisions are based on the evidence but also are influenced by values and resources. Moncrieff and Kirsch make clear where their values lie—antidepressants bad, psychological therapies good. But when criticising

Summary points

Recent meta-analyses show selective serotonin reuptake inhibitors have no clinically meaningful advantage over placebo

Claims that antidepressants are more effective in more severe conditions have little evidence to support them

Methodological artefacts may account for the small degree of superiority shown over placebo

Antidepressants have not been convincingly shown to affect the long term outcome of depression or suicide rates

Given doubt about their benefits and concern about their risks, current recommendations for prescribing antidepressants should be reconsidered

can have antidepressant effects, suggesting that these effects may be attributable to non-specific pharmacological or psychological mechanisms.[w10]

Effect of antidepressants

Longitudinal follow-up studies show very poor

convincing evidence of benefit. In children, the balance of benefits to risks is now recognised as unfavourable. We suggest this may also be the case for adults, given the continuing uncertainty about the possible risk of increased suicidality as well as other known adverse effects. This conclusion implies the need for a thorough re-evaluation of current approaches to depression and further development of alternatives to drug treatment. Since antidepressants have become society's main response to distress, expectations raised by decades of their use will also need to be addressed.

We thank other members of the Critical Psychiatry Network who contributed to the response to the NICE depression review and especially Duncan Double, who coordinated the response.

Contributors and sources: Both authors have conducted separate meta-analyses of antidepressant trials and reviews of antidepressant literature. JM has recently obtained an MD in antidepressant research methodology. The article draws on these sources, as well as the data contained in the NICE review. JM and IK contributed to the response to the NICE review. JM had the idea to write the paper. JM and IK drafted and revised the current manuscript. JM will act as guarantor.

Competing interests: IK has received consulting fees from Squibb and Pfizer. JM is co-chair of the Critical Psychiatry Network.

1 National Institute for Clinical Excellence. *Depression: management of depression in primary and secondary care. Clinical practice guideline No 23.* London: NICE, 2004. www.nice.org.uk/page.aspx?o = 235213 (accessed 24 May 2005).

2 Middleton H, Shaw I, Feder G. NICE guidelines for the management of depression. *BMJ* 2005;330:267-8.

3 Kirsch I, St John's wort, conventional medication, and placebo: an

Severity of depression

A key claim in the NICE guideline is that the superiority of antidepressants over placebo correlates positively with the severity of depression being treated. This belief is an old one. In 1958 Kuhn suggested that endogenous depression was more responsive to antidepressants than neurotic or reactive depression, which was generally regarded as less severe.[7] Regression to the mean may account for this impression since it entails that people with more severe depression at baseline will show greatest overall levels of improvement. But it does not explain drug-placebo differences, because greater improvement among patients with more severe depression occurs regardless of whether they are treated with a drug or placebo.

An early review of controlled trials found that evidence about whether endogenous symptoms predicted response was inconsistent.[8] Recent evidence comes from post-hoc analysis in trials with otherwise negative results[w6 w7] and from meta-analyses. The meta-analysis by Angst et al is often cited in support of the severity hypothesis, but severity effects were weak and mostly non-significant.[9] Effects in another meta-analysis were more impressive, but data were provided only for investigational antidepressants and not established ones, where the evidence seemed to be weaker.[10] In contrast, another recent meta-analysis found no relation between severity and antidepressant effect,[11] and a meta-analysis of older studies showed that differences between antidepressants and placebo were

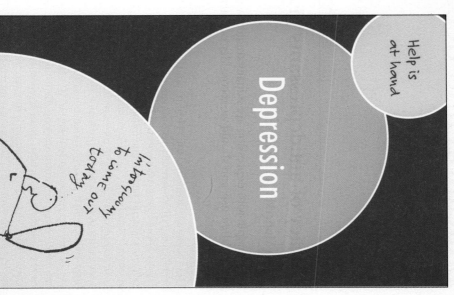

Education and debate

Efficacy of antidepressants in adults

Joanna Moncrieff, Irving Kirsch

Most people with depression are initially treated with antidepressants. But how well do the data support their use, and should we reconsider our strategy?

The National Institute for Health and Clinical Excellence (NICE) recently recommended that antidepressants, in particular selective serotonin reuptake inhibitors, should be first line treatment for moderate or severe depression.[1] This conclusion has broadly been accepted as valid.[2] The message is essentially the same as that of the Defeat Depression Campaign in the early 1990s, which probably contributed to the 253% rise in antidepressant prescribing in 10 years.[1] From our involvement in commenting on the evidence base for the guideline we believe these recommendations ignore NICE data. The continuing concern that selective serotonin reuptake inhibitors may increase the risk of suicidal behaviour[w1 w2] means there needs to be

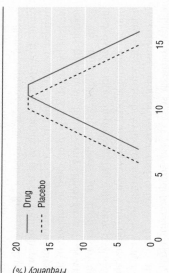

Normal distribution of scores for Hamilton rating scale for

Department of Mental Health Sciences, University College London, London W1N 8AA
Joanna Moncrieff
senior lecturer in social and community psychiatry

School of Health and Social work, University of Plymouth, Plymouth
Irving Kirsch
professor of psychology
Correspondence to:

further consideration or evidence for the efficacy of antidepressants in adults as there has been in children.

Efficacy

Although the NICE meta-analysis of placebo controlled trials of selective serotonin reuptake inhibitors found significant differences in levels of symptoms, these were so small that the effects were deemed unlikely to be clinically important.[1] The conclusion that the drugs had clinically important benefits was based on analysis of response and remission rates. However, in our comments on the draft guidelines, we pointed out that these categorical outcomes were derived from the same continuous data for symptoms scores that were found to show no clinically relevant effects. As NICE notes, "dichotomising scores into remission and non-remission creates an artificial boundary, with patients just over the cut-off score often being clinically indistinguishable from those just under the cut-off."[1]

The hypothetical data in the figure show how small differences may be magnified by transformation of continuous data into categorical data.[3] In this example, response was defined as a minimum 12 point improvement on the Hamilton rating scale for depression. Difference in mean change of scores between drug and placebo groups was 1 point. This scenario yields response rates of 50% in the drug condition and 32% in the placebo condition. Thus, if improvement is normally distributed and the criterion for response is close to the mean improvement rate (which it generally is), a very small difference in symptom score can push a large proportion of patients into different categories.

The small effects found on continuous measures are consistent with results of other recent meta-analyses of symptom scores. Khan et al found a 10% difference in levels of symptoms in two meta-analyses,[4 5] and Kirsch et al included unpublished studies in their latest analysis and found an overall mean difference of 1.7 points on the Hamilton scale.[6] No research evidence or consensus is available about what constitutes a clinically meaningful difference in Hamilton scores, but it seems unlikely that a difference of less than 2 points could be considered meaningful. NICE required a difference of at least 3 points as the criterion for clinical importance but gave no justification for this figure.[1] The most commonly used 17 item version of the Hamilton scale has a maximum score of 52 and contains seven items concerning sleep and anxiety, with each item on sleep scoring up to 6 points. Hence any drug with some sedative properties, including many antidepressants, could produce a difference of 2 points or more without exerting any specific antidepressant effect. Other recent meta-analyses that present categorical outcomes also find modest differences of between 14% and 18% in improvement or response rates.[w3-w5]

References w1-w20 are on bmj.com

depression with mean score of 11.5 for antidepressant and 10.5 for placebo

j.moncrieff@ucl.ac.uk

BMJ 2005;331:155-9

pared with outpatient trials.[12] The NICE meta-analysis failed to find a consistent gradient of effect from "moderate" (Hamilton score 14-18) through "severe" (19-22) to "very severe" depression (≥23).[1] In fact, the middle group, which would generally be referred to as moderately depressed, tended to show larger effects than either of the other two, but numbers of studies were small.

Thus there seems to be little support for the suggestion that recent failure to find marked differences between antidepressants and placebo is due to recruitment of patients with mild depression that is less responsive to antidepressants.[1] Indeed, in the meta-analysis by Kirsch et al, all but one of the trials were conducted in patients with severe to very severe depression according to NICE criteria.[6] The possibility that patients in the mid-range of severity show a greater antidepressant response, as suggested by the NICE data and by Joyce and Paykel,[8] would not be expected from a simple biological effect. It may indicate that this group is more susceptible to some methodological artefact such as infringement of the double blind (see below).

Methodological issues in antidepressant trials

Several commentators have suggested that the small effects of antidepressants compared with placebos may be attributable to methodological factors or selective presentation of data from antidepressant trials.[w8-w10] These include concerns that trials of antidepressants may not be truly double blind. This is because

participants may be able to detect differences between placebos and drugs because the drugs cause noticeable physiological effects including, but not limited to, recognised side effects. Other concerns include the validity of outcome measures, that discontinuation effects may confound continuation trials, and that results may be inflated by exclusion of people who withdraw early from the analysis. Evidence also shows that trials of antidepressants with negative results are less likely to be published than those with positive results and that, within published trials, negative outcomes may not be presented.[13]

A neglected aspect of antidepressant trials is the substantial heterogeneity of their findings.[12] Although many trials do find antidepressants are superior to placebo, many do not, including some of the largest and most well known landmark trials such as the Medical Research Council trial and the early National Institute for Mental Health trial.[w11 w12] In addition, many trials find that substances as diverse as methylphenidate, benzodiazepines, and antipsychotics

The Royal College of Psychiatrists

Campaigns raising awareness of depression have contributed to increased prescribing of antidepressants hospital[14] and in the community,[15] and the overall prevalence of depression is rising despite increased use of antidepressants.[16] Two studies that prospectively assessed outcome in depressed patients treated naturalistically by general practitioners and psychiatrists found that people prescribed antidepressants had a slightly worse outcome than those not prescribed them, even after baseline severity had been taken into account.[17 18] No comparable studies could be found that showed a better outcome in people prescribed antidepressants.

Some authors have suggested a causal association between increased antidepressant prescribing since 1990 and reduction of overall suicide rates observed in some countries.[w13 w14] However, others have pointed out that falls in overall suicide rates started long before this period,[w15-w17] and suicide rates have increased in some age groups[w18] and some countries[w18] despite increased antidepressant prescribing. Meta-analyses of data from controlled trials have not found reduced rates of suicide or suicidal behaviour in drug arms compared with placebo arms.[4 5 w19 w20]

Conclusions

The NICE review data suggest that selective serotonin reuptake inhibitors do not have a clinically meaningful advantage over placebo, which is consistent with other recent meta-analyses. In addition, methodological artefacts may account for the small effect seen. Evidence that antidepressants are more effective in more severe conditions is not strong, and data on long term outcome of depression and suicide do not provide

4 Khan A, Warner HA, Brown WA. Symptom reduction and suicide risk in patients treated with placebo in antidepressant clinical trials. Arch Gen Psychiatry 2000;57:311-24.

5 Khan A, Khan SR, Leventhal RM, Brown WA. Symptom reduction and suicide risk in patients treated with placebo antidepressant clinical trials: a replication analysis of the Food and Administration Database. Int J Neuropsychopharmacol 2001;2:113-8.

6 Kirsch I, Moore TJ, Scoboria A. Nicholls SS. The emperor's new drugs: an analysis of antidepressant medication data submitted to the US Food and Drug Administration. Prev Treat 2002;5.www.journals.apa.org/prevention/volume5/pre050023a.html (accessed 20 May 2005).

7 Kuhn R. The treatment of depressive states with G22355 (imipramine hydrochloride). Am J Psychiatry 1958;115:459-64.

8 Joyce PR, Paykel ES. Predictors of drug response in depression. Arch Gen Psychiatry 1989;46:89-99.

9 Angst J, Scheidegger P, Stabl M. Efficacy of moclobemide in different patient groups: results of new subscales of the Hamilton Rating Scale. Clin Neuropharmacol 1993;16 (suppl 2):S55-62.

10 Khan A, Leventhal RM, Khan SR, Brown WA. Severity of depression and response to antidepressants and placebo: An analysis of the Food and Drug Administration database. J Clin Psychopharmacol 2002;22:40-5.

11 Kirsch I, Scoboria A, Moore TJ. Antidepressants and placebos: secrets, revelations, and unanswered questions. Prev Treat 2002;5. www.journals.apa.org/prevention/volume5/pre050033r.html (accessed 20 May 2005).

12 Moncrieff J. A comparison of antidepressant trials using active and inert placebos. Int J Methods Psychiatric Res 2003;12:117-27.

13 Melander H, Ahlqvist-Rastad J, Meijer G, Beermann B. Evidence b(i)ased medicine—selective reporting from studies sponsored by pharmaceutical industry: review of studies in new drug applications. BMJ 2003;326:1171-3.

14 Tuma TA. Outcome of hospital treated depression at 4.5 years. An elderly and a younger cohort compared. Br J Psychiatry 2000;176:224-8.

15 Goldberg D, Privett M, Ustun B, Simon G, Linden M. The effects of detection and treatment on the outcome of major depression in primary care: a naturalistic study in 15 cities. Br J Gen Pract 1998;48:1840-4.

16 Fombonne E. Increased rates of depression: update of epidemiological findings and analytical problems. Acta Psychiatr Scand 1994;90:145-56.

17 Brugha TS, Bebbington P, MacCarthy B, Stuart E, Wykes T. Antidepressants may not assist recovery in practice: a naturalistic prospective survey. Acta Psychiatr Scand 1992;86:5-11.

18 Ronalds C, Creed F, Stone K, Webb S, Tomenson B. The outcome of anxiety and depressive disorders in general practice. Br J Psychiatry 1997;171:427-33.

(Accepted 11 May 2005)

randomised controlled trials, so the trials are often small and the people who participate are not representative of the wider population of depressed people. Decisions about treatment are based on adverse effects as well as benefits, yet randomised controlled trials are poor at detecting rare but important adverse effects. In the recent debate about selective serotonin reuptake inhibitors in children, it wasn't effectiveness that was the issue but suicide.

Competing interests: None declared.

1 Moncrieff J, Kirsch I. Efficiency of antidepressant activity in adults. *BMJ* 2005;331:155-7.
2 Parker G. Evaluating treatments for the mood disorders: time for the evidence to get real. *Aust N Z J Psychiatry* 2004;38:408-14.
3 Safer DJ. Design and reporting modifications in industry-sponsored comparative psychopharmacology trials. *J Nerv Ment Dis* 2002;190:583-92.
4 Gilbody S, Song F. Publication bias and the integrity of psychiatric research. *Psychol Med* 2000;30:253-8.
5 Black N. Why we need observational studies to evaluate the effectiveness of health care. *BMJ* 1996;312:1215-8.

One hundred years ago
Medical advice gratis

As newspapers, from the *Times* downwards, are seeking for outside attractions in order to maintain their circulation, it is not surprising to find that *Answers* announces that it is ready to place at the disposal of its readers in return for one year's subscription the right to consult "our staff of doctors" who are said to be part of "a fully equipped staff of brilliant specialists in every field of human activity." This is not quite so cheap as a gift with a pound of tea, but yet is an economical way of obtaining medical advice if we consider that the annual subscription amounts only to 4s. 6d., and that there is no limit to the number of times each subscriber may seek advice, the only drawback being that "consultations" are through the post. We should like to know who are the medical practitioners who render assistance in this way and to what class in the profession they belong. Consultations by post are unscientific and ought to be condemned by medical opinion, as the only information upon which the recipient of the letter acts is the statement of the patient, unless this is supplemented by secretions sent for examination, but even then the risks of mistakes are too great to make the practice safe. There is a more serious aspect of the question which should not be overlooked. Although the practitioners who undertake this work are not advertised by name, the system is in effect advertising for practice, and all patients who come to them through the newspaper are obtained by advertising; therefore it would be in accordance with the principles upon which the General Medical Council has acted if such practice were to be regarded with the same disfavour as that of the Medical Aid Societies which advertise and canvass to procure patients.

(*BMJ* 1905;ii:1472)

4   Davenport RJ, Dennis MS, Warlow CP. Effect of correcting outcome data for case mix: an example from stroke medicine. *Br Med J* 1996; **312**: 1503–5.
5   Wolfe C, Beech R, Ratcliffe M, Rudd AG. Stroke care in Europe. Can we learn lessons from the different ways stroke is managed in different countries? Review. *J R Soc Health* 1995; **115**: 143–7.
6   Wolfe CD, Tilling K, Beech R, Rudd AG. Variations in case fatality and dependency from stroke in western and central Europe. The European BIOMED Study of Stroke Care Group. *Stroke* 1999; **30**: 350–6.

8 | Issues raised by the national sentinel audit for stroke

Jonathan Mant
Senior Lecturer, University of Birmingham

The national sentinel audit for stroke (NSAS) provided important information. It highlighted evidence of deficiencies in how stroke patients are treated in the UK, and demonstrated wide variations in standards of care.[1] In considering how to measure the quality of care for older people more broadly, it is useful to reflect on the factors that contributed to the success of the NSAS. In the design of any study such as this, the investigators need to make a number of choices (Table 1) on a number of issues, each of which has pros and cons, and there are no 'right' or 'wrong' answers.

Confidentiality versus accountability

The first issue is that the NSAS was *confidential*. This was probably an important factor contributing to its success, in terms both of response rate (80% of trusts that care for acute stroke patients) and of its ability to identify problems. Units that performed badly were not identified in the published report, which raises the issue of *accountability*. Does the public have a right to know if the local hospitals are performing poorly? On the one hand, by keeping the identity of trusts confidential, a potentially powerful lever for change is lost; on the other, if the data are not

Table 1. Audit design: choices that need to be made.

- Confidentiality vs accountability
- National picture vs local picture
- Pragmatism vs methodological purity
- Document vs doing
- Episodic vs continuous data collection
- Process vs outcome data
- Whose responsibility is it to take action?

anonymised, there is the risk that the results will become distorted and unreliable as trusts try to avoid being identified as 'bad apples'.[2]

National versus local picture

The second issue is that the emphasis of the NSAS report was on the poor standards of stroke care *nationally*, rather than focusing on *local* problems. This was probably appropriate, given the way the data were collected – by local trust staff from a variety of disciplines using an audit proforma with explanatory notes. It is likely that different people interpreting the forms in different ways will have produced some variation between localities (although, in fact, agreement between raters within a trust tended to be good).[1] In addition, because no more than 40 patients were included from each trust, there will have been a degree of random variation in the results at trust level. Therefore, the data are more robust when interpreted at national rather than local level.

The emphasis on the national results was picked up by the press, which reported the results of the audit as a national issue rather than as a series of local problems. For example, the *News of the World* reported that only 40% of hospitals bother to weigh their patients.[3] This is a more comfortable situation for the hospitals, since national solutions and scapegoats tend to be sought rather than local ones. Thus, the *News of the World* viewed it as a problem for the Health Secretary, Alan Milburn, and recommended that he should 'issue instructions from the top'.[3]

Pragmatism versus methodological purity

The third issue is that the design of the audit was *pragmatic* rather than being *methodologically pure*. As discussed in Chapter 7, there were a number of weaknesses in the design. Case identification relied on the use of routine information systems, which is an adequate but not ideal method of identifying patients admitted with acute stroke. For example, in one study such an approach was found to miss 12% of stroke patients and include an extra 28% who had not had a stroke.[4] The audit was performed using a retrospective case note review rather than prospectively recording data, so is heavily dependent upon the quality of the case notes. Nevertheless, these and the other study limitations are justified in that the audit was successfully completed. There is a trade-off in any study between eliminating all potential sources of bias and error and designing a feasible and affordable approach. The key point is that the results need to be interpreted, as they were in this case, in the light of any methodological limitations.

Document versus doing

Fourthly, the NSAS was concerned with recording what was *documented* in case notes, not with what was actually *done*. This is a pragmatic approach, but what is documented is not the same as what is done and does not necessarily inform as to whether something has been done properly. Case note documentation is important – indeed, from a medico-legal point of view, it is essential – but quality of care is not the same as quality of case notes! Furthermore, there is a danger that healthcare staff can become over preoccupied with documentation, and not notice what is actually happening. Therefore, in audits (especially prospective ones) it is important to prioritise data collection, and collect only those data regarded as essential, rather than collect data because they might be useful.

Episodic versus continuous data collection

A fifth issue is whether data should be collected on an *episodic* or a *continuous* basis. The NSAS was an example of an episodic audit, in that data were collected over a three-month period, with the implicit understanding that data collection was likely to be repeated at a future date. The alternative is to set up a system that allows for continuous data collection. Both approaches have a role. In practice, monitoring involving continuous data collection relies on data that can be obtained from routine information systems and, as such, reflects what is available rather than what is important from a quality of care perspective. It is possible to add data items to routine information systems, whether at trust or department level (eg stroke registers), so audit of 'important' items can switch from episodic to continuous. In making a decision as to whether this is worth doing, it is relevant to consider the likelihood that standards in units will change significantly over time. For example, if a unit initially performs poorly on a specific component of care (eg proportion of patients who have had a swallowing assessment), it is likely that continuous monitoring will be worthwhile, since this area has been demonstrated to be an important quality monitoring issue. Once a high standard has been achieved, it may be that other areas become more pressing priorities for monitoring. Flexibility is needed, since what is perceived as important to monitor will change over time.

Process versus outcome data

Sixthly, the NSAS chose to focus on *process* of care (eg what tests were carried out during the first 24 hours) rather than on its *outcome* (eg mortality rate). The relative merits of process as opposed to outcome measures are discussed in earlier chapters. In general, process measures are less controversial, easier to interpret, require smaller numbers to audit, are less prone to data distortions, and case mix adjustments are less crucial.[5] Thus, audits based around process of care are likely to be cheaper and easier to make use of as a means of improving quality of care. However, their validity depends upon a proven link existing between process and outcome and, from a public perspective, it may be that audits of outcome are of greater interest. A statement that more patients are dying in hospital A than in hospital B has greater immediacy than a statement that patients in hospital A are less likely to be weighed. The danger is that a simplistic cause and effect relationship is assumed (more people die in hospital A, so it must be worse), rather than alternative explanations (chance, variations in how the data were collected or differences in case mix). In general, monitoring outcome is likely to be most useful where differences in quality of care are likely to lead to measurable differences in outcome. Optimal care of stroke patients can lead to detectable differences in outcome in large studies: organised stroke unit care results in a 17% reduction in death at one year compared with conventional care.[6] However, such mortality differences are unlikely to be detectable in non-randomised audits once the effects of case mix have been taken into account.[7]

Whose responsibility is it to take action?

Finally, on the basis that the underlying aim of audit is to improve the quality of care, it is important to consider *whose responsibility* it is to take action on the results. This can be considered at many levels, including the Secretary of State for Health, the NHS Executive, commissioners of healthcare, including health authorities and primary care groups, trust management, clinicians, patients and the public. These several players will have different contributions to make, depending upon the perceived nature of any problems and the proposed solutions. It is important that perspectives on responsibility remain broad and inclusive.

Conclusion

In summary, the NSAS not only provides a valuable snapshot of the quality of inpatient care for stroke in the UK, but it also offers lessons on how audits might be applied in other areas of healthcare for older people. The choices made in the design of the NSAS may not be appropriate in all areas, but the issues summarised in Table 1 offer a useful framework to consider for any quality of care topic.

References

1   Rudd AG, Irwin P, Rutledge Z, Lowe D, *et al.* The national sentinel audit for stroke: a tool for raising standards of care. *J R Coll Physicians Lond* 1999; **33**: 460–4.

2   Berwick DM. Continuous improvement as an ideal in healthcare. *N Engl J Med* 1989; **320**: 53–6.

3   Parry V. Time for action at a stroke. *News of the World*, 17 October 1999.

4   Mant J, Mant F, Winner S. How good is routine information? Validation of coding for acute stroke in Oxford hospitals. *Health Trends* 1989; **29**: 96–9.

5   Mant J, Hicks N. Detecting differences in quality of care: the sensitivity of measures of process and outcome in treating acute myocardial infarction. *Br Med J* 1995; **311**: 793–6.

6   Stroke Unit Trialists' Collaboration. *Organised in-patient (stroke unit) care for stroke.* (Cochrane Review). In: The Cochrane Library, Issue 4, 1999. Oxford: Software Update.

7   Davenport RJ, Dennis MS, Warlow CP. Effect of correcting outcome data for case mix: an example from stroke medicine. *Br Med J* 1996; **312**: 1503–5.

9 | Urinary incontinence: audit study using health outcome indicators

Jonathan Potter
Associate Director, Clinical Effectiveness and Evaluation Unit,
Royal College of Physicians

Background

The urinary incontinence audit contrasts with the previous studies on fractured femur and stroke. The former was a large-scale analysis of hospital activity records over many years with no recourse to hospital notes, while the stroke study was a national audit at hospital level with retrospective review of hospital notes by audit staff. The current study is smaller in scale, with data collected at ward or care setting level. The methodological differences between the studies permit some analysis and discussion of the difficulties with regard to data collection and data analysis, together with an evaluation of the reliability, validity and acceptability of the data.

The study was designed to investigate the usefulness of health outcome indicators for incontinence. The outcome indicators have been developed by the National Centre for Health Outcomes Development (NCHOD).[1] Details of the methods by which they were derived have been described in Chapter 5. Such indicators do not necessarily define what is good or bad practice, but point to those areas that might benefit from review. Of the 18 indicators for incontinence developed by an expert working party under the chairmanship of Professor Brocklehurst, three were relevant to long-term care settings:[1]

1 *The prevalence of urinary incontinence* may be used as an outcome measure to monitor the quality of assessment and treatment of urinary incontinence.

2 *The use of indwelling catheters* may also be used as an outcome measure to monitor the quality of management of urinary incontinence. A low prevalence of indwelling urinary catheters should arguably be expected if incontinence is being properly assessed, treated and managed.

3 *The clinical assessment rate* provides a process measure of the clinical management of incontinence.

Method

The study included 1,125 residents (of whom 608 were incontinent) in 17 residential homes, 13 nursing homes and five long-stay wards. Data were collected as a cross-sectional snapshot using the Royal College of Physicians CARE scheme.[2] This is an audit tool designed to evaluate the quality of care in long-term care settings, developed by Professor Brocklehurst and validated in field studies. Staff in the care settings collected the data based on information from medical records and local clinical knowledge of residents. In addition to collecting data for the three outcome measures, a questionnaire was sent to each participating centre to obtain feedback about the validity, reliability, feasibility and acceptability of the outcome indicators.

Results

Prevalence of urinary incontinence

The prevalence rates for urinary incontinence are shown in Table 1. The high burden of urinary incontinence is demonstrated by rates of up to 71% in nursing homes and long-stay wards. The prevalence rates for urinary incontinence within sites in each setting are shown in Fig 1. The results demonstrate great variability. Such variation may reflect differences in the quality of care or result from confounding influences such as case mix, differences in admission policy or difficulties with the definition and identification of subjects in different settings.

In order to assess the issue of case mix in more detail, the data have been further analysed. First, they were examined to establish whether correlations existed between incontinence and case mix factors such as age, gender, confusional state and functional ability. There was no correlation with age or gender, but there were obvious strong correlations

Table 1. The prevalence rates for urinary incontinence in long-term care settings.

Long-term care facility	Total	Total incontinent	Prevalence of incontinence (%)
Residential	504	170	34
Nursing	508	358	71
Long-stay hospitals	113	80	71
Total	1,125	608	54

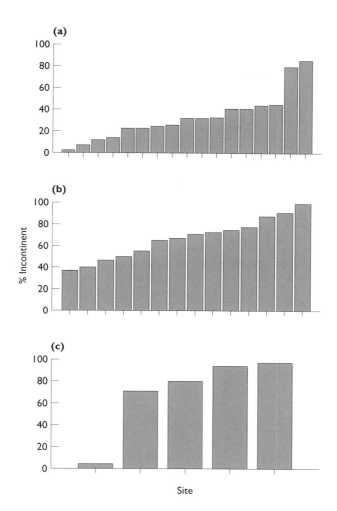

Fig 1. *Prevalence of incontinence in* (**a**) *residential homes,* (**b**) *nursing homes and* (**c**) *long-stay wards.*

with dependency using the Barthel score (Mann Whitney *p* = 0.001), and with confusional state measured by the Abbreviated Mental Test (chi-square *p* < 0.001).

Secondly, the prevalence of these case mix factors was assessed in each of the care settings. In long-stay wards, the prevalence of severe/very severe dependency (Fig 2) and confusion (Fig 3) was consistently high. These results demonstrate the marked variation between settings in the prevalence of risks factors for incontinence. Such case mix variation will influence the prevalence of incontinence, and thus make interpretation of this health outcome indicator difficult.

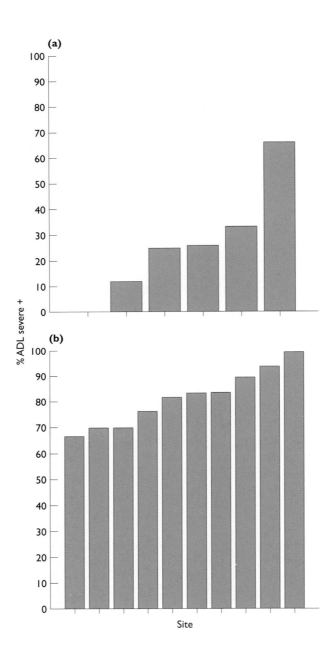

Fig 2. *Percentage with severe (Barthel score 0–3) or very severe (Barthel 4–6) dependency in* **(a)** *residential and* **(b)** *nursing homes* (ADL = activities of daily living; 'severe +' = severe or very severe dependency).

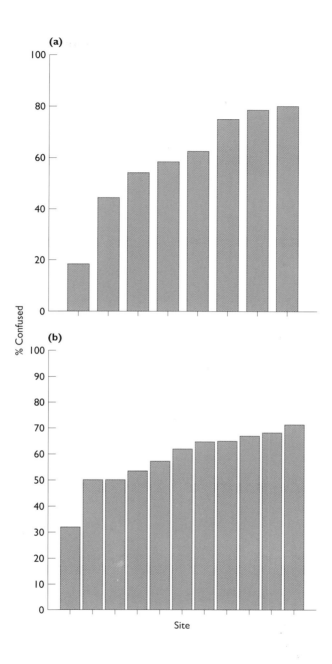

Fig 3. *Percentage of subjects with confusional states in* **(a)** *residential and* **(b)** *nursing homes* (confusional state as defined within the CARE scheme[2]).

Use of indwelling urethral catheters

The prevalence of indwelling catheters among the incontinent subjects in different settings is shown in Fig 4. There is a marked variation between settings, with rates varying from 0–20% in residential homes and long-stay wards and from 0–40% in nursing homes. These rates reflect differences in management protocols used within settings. It is accepted that a degree of indwelling catheter use may be acceptable, but anything other than a very low rate suggests that review of practice may be required.

The relationship between the prevalence of incontinence and the

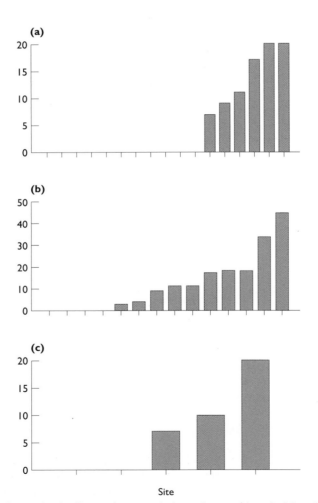

Fig 4. *Prevalence of indwelling catheter use in incontinent subjects in* **(a)** *residential care,* **(b)** *nursing homes and* **(c)** *long-stay wards.*

prevalence of indwelling catheters is shown in Fig 5. It is noticeable that many units have a high rate of incontinence but a low rate of indwelling catheterisation, which suggests good practice. Equally, there are units with a high rate of indwelling catheterisation despite a low prevalence of urinary incontinence, indicating the need for a review of their practices for the management of urinary incontinence.

Case mix may also influence the use of indwelling catheters as a more dependent group of subjects might be expected to require catheterisation more than a less dependent group. The relationship between dependency and use of indwelling catheters in long-term care settings is shown in Table 2. The need for indwelling catheters may be justified in some highly dependent subjects. The results suggest that a review of policies would be appropriate where catheters are used in moderately or mildly dependent subjects, and also in care settings where a high number of subjects require catheterisation (ie nursing homes).

The prevalence of use of urethral indwelling catheters provides a

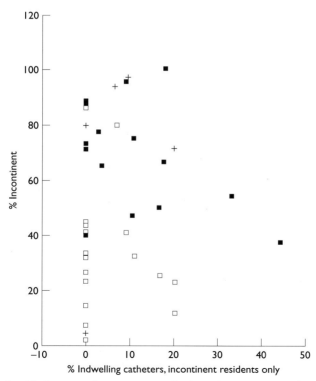

Fig 5. *Relationship between the percentage of urinary incontinence and the percentage with indwelling catheters in different care settings (□ = residential, ■ = nursing homes, + = long-stay wards).*

Table 2. The relationship between dependency and the use of indwelling catheters in long-term care settings.

Long-term care facility	Dependency			
	Very severe	Severe	Moderate	Mild
Residential	1	1	0	1
Nursing	25	8	2	1
Long-stay hospital	1	0	0	0

potentially useful outcome indicator for the management of urinary incontinence. The results identify care settings in which management protocols for urinary incontinence might be reviewed to improve practice and the quality of care.

Clinical assessment

The third outcome indicator, clinical assessment rate, is a process measure of quality. The audit sought details about the process of assessment and management of subjects with incontinence. Details of information sought are shown in Tables 3 and 4. However, the process details are poorly defined and open to differences in interpretation. Thus, categories such as 'full assessment' within 'details of management plan' (Table 4) could be interpreted or recorded in various ways. For example, what is a full assessment? Some details of a full assessment may have been carried out but not recorded in the notes.

Table 3. Details and frequency of assessment plan recorded.

Assessment plan	RH (%)	NH (%)	Long-stay hospital (%)	Total	
				%	No.
Relevant history	94	73	96	82	490/598
Relevant examination	62	44	44	49	282/578
Cause of incontinence	59	52	77	57	335/588
Management plan	81	67	78	72	429/592

NH = nursing home; RH = residential home.

Table 4. Details and frequency of management plan recorded.

Management plan	RH (%)	NH (%)	Long-stay hospital (%)	Total %	No.
Carried out	84	63	77	70	402/573
Effectiveness	81	59	60	65	376/577
No assessment	4	14	3		
Full assessment	48	24	36		

NH = nursing home; RH = residential home.

Two process measures, relevant examination (Fig 6) and treatment of infection (Fig 7), were selected to compare process measures in the different settings. Considerable variation was found between the settings for both parameters. While this may reflect differences in the process of assessment and management, and hence in the quality of care, there may also be methodological difficulties which explain the variations seen between settings. What is a 'relevant examination' needs more definition. Precise guidelines are required about what constitutes such an examination. Are details of the examination recorded? An examination may have been carried out but details not noted, or an examination may have been carried out but may not have been effective. Alternatively, the results of an examination may have been recorded, but the information may be difficult to find or retrieve from the records.

Similarly, questions could also apply to the treatment of infection. For example, what constitutes treatment, and was this a valid measure to record at the time? There may be no infection requiring treatment.

Such difficulties will inevitably result in contrasting information and results from differing centres.

Questionnaire survey

A questionnaire sent to participating pilot sites sought feedback with regard to the validity, feasibility and acceptability of the study. The replies are summarised below.

Validity

Contributors to the audit felt that the outcome indicators were valid and a fair way to assess practice. There was also a general acceptance that the

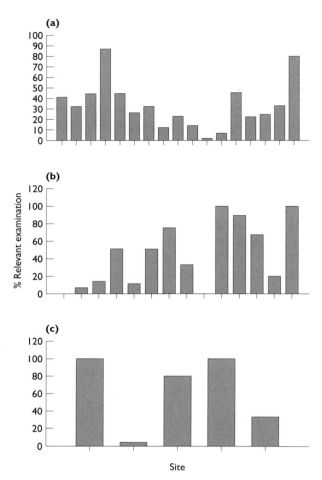

Fig 6. *Percentage with relevant examination in* **(a)** *residential homes,* **(b)** *nursing homes and* **(c)** *long-stay wards.*

measures were useful within sites. Concerns were expressed over the method of selecting sites for study. The results reflect the standards in centres that may already be interested in high standards and are therefore prepared to be audited. It is possible that results may be significantly better in these centres than the standards currently in existence within the service overall.

Feasibility

Contributors felt that the data collection was straightforward. It could be managed on a ward basis with data collected by staff. The data required

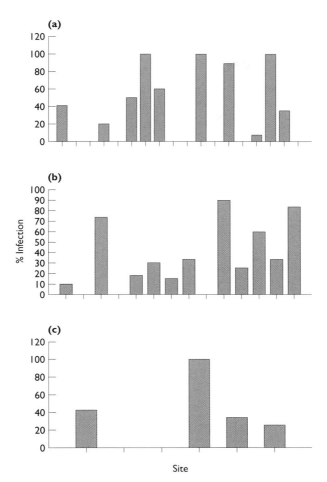

Fig 7. *Treatment of infection in* (**a**) *residential homes,* (**b**) *nursing homes and* (**c**) *long-stay wards.*

were easily available either from the records or from the knowledge of staff working with the subjects. The amount of information sought was also thought reasonable. In some settings, there were concerns about the collection of specific items such as the Barthel score. There was felt to be a need for training to ensure accurate and reproducible data collection.

Acceptability

Contributors found the data extremely useful at local level for professional development of staff, monitoring standards, feedback to staff and for changing practice. There was, however, much concern about the use of the data for comparisons between units, and also an awareness of marked variations between settings relating to issues of selection and case mix. It was generally felt that any interpretation of the comparative data should be undertaken only by those with an understanding of the limitations of such analyses.

Conclusion

Health outcome indicators have been developed by an expert working group on behalf of NCHOD. Three of these indicators have been piloted in long-term care settings. The collection of data at local level proved feasible and was generally appreciated by participating sites.

The pilot study has demonstrated the methodological difficulties in collecting data for indicators of quality of care. Two indicators proved highly variable in practice, and would require further refinement before use as a comparative measure. The study of indwelling urethral catheter use demonstrates potential as an outcome measure providing an indication of the quality of care. In order to utilise other measures of quality, there will need to be more systematic collection of data to give an indication of case mix, and more precise definitions of terms to allow the consistent and objective collection of process information.

Participating centres found the use of the outcome indicators helpful at local level for monitoring and improving services. Most groups, however, agreed that the indicators should not be used as a comparative measure of quality until further refined and better understood.

The study demonstrates the challenge that still exists in collecting data to provide comparative information about the quality of care for older people. It is essential that these methodological issues are addressed if clinicians are to have confidence in the use of health outcome indicators as a measure of the quality of service.

References

1   Brocklehurst J, Amess M, Goldacre M, Mason A, *et al* (eds). *Health outcome indicators for urinary incontinence. Report of a working group to the Department of Health.* Oxford: National Centre for Health Outcomes Development, 1999.

2   Dickinson E, Brocklehurst J. *The CARE scheme: clinical audit of long-term care of elderly people.* London: Royal College of Physicians of London, 1999.

10 | Standardised assessment and aggregated databases: alternative approaches to measuring the quality of care

Iain Carpenter

Senior Lecturer, Centre for Health Services Studies, University of Kent at Canterbury; Department of Health Care of the Elderly, Guy's, King's and St Thomas' Medical School, London; Honorary Consultant, Kent & Canterbury Hospital, Canterbury

One of the greatest challenges in the care of older people is the lack of routinely available data appropriate for evaluating the quality and outcome of their care. Acute hospital activity data (using the contract minimum data set) form the basis of the performance indicators that broadly apply to the evaluation of services for people admitted to hospital with acute illnesses. However, because illness in older people is characterised by multiple impairments and chronic diseases, these indicators are less useful for evaluation of their care in post-acute and rehabilitation settings and of no use for continuing care in community or institutional settings. The Department of Health National Beds Enquiry[1] recommendations to provide more care for older people outside hospital in intermediate care settings give added importance to finding an acceptable solution to this problem. The recommendations state that:

> There would be an active policy to build up intermediate care services (ie services designed to prevent avoidable admissions to acute care settings and to facilitate the transition from hospital to home and from medical dependence to functional independence). There would be a major expansion of both community health and social care services. In contrast acute hospital services would be focused on rapid assessment, stabilisation and treatment. Hospital day units and community based services would be aimed at maintaining people in their home communities in good health, preventing avoidable admissions, facilitating early discharge and active rehabilitation post-discharge and supporting a return to normal community-based living wherever possible. Over time 'places' in community schemes might replace some acute hospital beds.

Any moves in this direction must be accompanied by focused attention on how appropriate data can be made routinely available to ensure that there is no deterioration in the quality of care.

This chapter provides two illustrations of how the problems could be addressed, based on the use of information generated by aggregating data from routine assessment of older people using standardised assessment instruments developed by an international research collaboration (www.interrai.org).

Quality of care report for a nursing home

Figure 1 shows a quality of care report for a nursing home using real data (but a fictitious facility name) from a database in the USA (the work of David Zimmerman and colleagues at the University of Wisconsin). The information is generated from routine assessments – conducted for care planning purposes – of all people admitted to nursing homes in the USA, made at admission and quarterly thereafter. The data are entered into a database holding assessment information that is anonymised except for the facility in which the old people are being cared. Thirty-one quality

Nursing Home Quality Indicators Profile

Facility Name: InterRAI Research and Rest Home

Report Period: 7/1/96 to 12/31/96

Domain/Quality Indicator	Number with QI	Number in Denominator	Facility Percentage	Peer Group Percentage	%ile Rank	Flag
Accidents						
1. Incidence of New Fracture	1	79	1.3%	1.8%	40	
2. Prevalence of Falls	14	79	17.7%	13.3%	81	
Behavioral/Emotional						
3. Prevalence of Behavioral Symptoms	21	79	26.6%	21.2%	76	
High Risk	19	56	33.9%	26.4%	79	
Low Risk	2	23	8.7%	10.2%	58	
4. Symptoms of Depression	23	79	29.1%	15.1%	91	⌐⌐
5. Symptoms of Depression without Antidepressant Therapy	13	79	16.5%	7.9%	93	⌐⌐
Clinical Management						
6. Use of 9+ Medications	22	79	27.8%	27.6%	52	
Cognitive Patterns						
7. Onset of Cognitive Impairment	1	24	4.2%	10.3%	19	

Fig 1. *Quality of care report* (reproduced by kind permission of Dr David Zimmerman; ©Center for Health Systems Research and Analysis, University of Wisconsin, Madison).

indicators (QIs) that can be used to monitor care at the level of the individual or the institution have been developed from these assessment items.[2] Examples of seven of them are shown in Fig 1. The columns in the report are constructed as follows:

▌ *Number with QI:* the number of residents with the QI (the number of residents in the numerator).

▌ *Number in denominator:* the number of residents in the nursing home for whom the indicator is relevant.

▌ *Facility percentage:* the percentage of residents for whom the indicator is relevant who have the indicator.

▌ *Peer group percentage:* the percentage of residents who have the indicator in a comparable group of nursing homes.

▌ *%ile rank:* the percentile rank of a home within the comparable group of nursing homes.

Prevalence of disturbed behavioural symptoms (Fig 1, indicator 3) is shown separately for those at high risk and those at low risk, as it is among people with significant cognitive impairment that behavioural problems are more common. Thus, 19 of 56 high risk and two of 23 low risk residents show behavioural symptoms. The ability to relate information on a QI to other information on the resident in this way gives greater precision in demonstrating quality of care as it is a means of case mix adjustment.

Some QIs are more critical than others. For example, it is probably more acceptable that 30% of residents of a nursing home should be incontinent of urine than that 30% of them have severe pressure sores. One way of setting acceptable prevalence rates is by comparing the performance of a given home with a comparable group of nursing homes. Fig 1 shows that 16.5% of the residents in this home have symptoms of depression without any antidepressant therapy (indicator 5) compared with 7.9% in comparable homes. This places the home in the bottom 10% (%ile rank 93) of the peer group. The indicator has therefore been flagged as it probably requires particular attention.

Standardised assessment of need in different settings

Introducing consistency in assessment opens further benefits when undertaken in different settings. Evaluating quality and patterns of care in institutional settings, although not easy, is considerably less difficult than the same task in community settings. Figs 2 and 3 illustrate what can be explored when comparable standardised assessment of need is undertaken across settings and the data aggregated.

These data have been taken from a number of studies evaluating a standardised assessment in the UK and are therefore not representative, but they illustrate points that would be important were they found to be generally true. The figures show data from five different populations (Table 1).

Activities of daily living

Fig 2 shows the number of activities of daily living (ADL) with which people require assistance. As would be expected, people discharged home

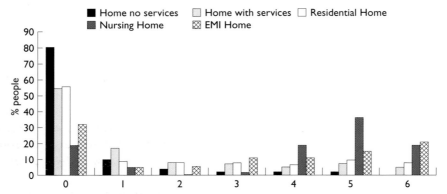

Fig 2. *Percentage of people who required assistance with differing numbers of activities of daily living (ADL): comparison of people at home and in institutional care.*

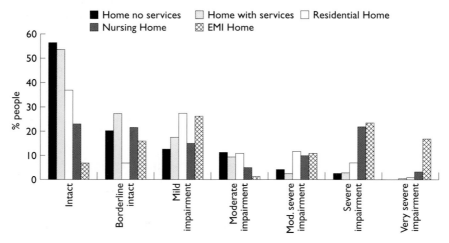

Fig 3. *Percentage of people with differing levels of cognitive ability as measured by the Minimum data set (MDS) Cognitive Performance Scale[3] score: comparison of people at home and in institutional care.*

Table 1. The populations from which data were taken for standardised assessment of need across settings.

1	Discharged home from rehabilitation wards without support services*
2	Discharged home with support services or assessed for services while at home**
3	Living in residential homes†
4	Living in nursing homes†
5	Living in EMI homes†

* From a project in four rehabilitation wards for the elderly in two hospitals in East Kent.
** From a project in social services departments in East Kent and South London.
† From a pilot study in residential and nursing homes around England.
EMI = elderly mentally infirm.

without support services require assistance with fewer ADL than people discharged with services or who are assessed for services in their own homes. People living in nursing homes and elderly mentally infirm (EMI) homes tend to be more physically disabled and require assistance with more ADL. There is little difference between those living in their own homes with services and those living in residential homes.

Cognitive impairment

Fig 3 shows the prevalence of cognitive impairment in the same populations using a cognitive performance scale generated from four of the assessment items.[3] It is measured without resort to use of a specific cognitive assessment instrument such as the Abbreviated Mental Test or the Mini Mental State Examination. Cognitive impairment is slightly more prevalent in people in the community receiving services than those discharged home without services. However, unlike the situation with ADL, cognitive impairment is more prevalent in residential home populations than in people living in their own homes. Perhaps of greater importance is the high prevalence of cognitive impairment in nursing homes. These nursing homes are not registered for managing people with cognitive impairment and dementia, even though the prevalence is not dissimilar to that shown for EMI homes. The relevance for quality of care is that, in spite of the high prevalence of cognitive impairment and dementia, staff in non-EMI homes generally have not had appropriate training in their recognition or management.

The other more likely peril is that, because dementia is not specifically recognised as a disorder, a culture has developed in non-EMI homes in which cognitive impairment is seen as an inevitable attribute of being old and in a home. This can lead to a systematic negation of all patients' choices, usually on safety grounds. Also, ignoring a high prevalence of dementia in non-EMI homes ignores the plight of older people *without* dementia in these homes. There is anecdotal evidence that the presence of many demented patients in the home is a source of great frustration and distress for the non-demented residents.

Evidence-based clinical practice: the future

The advent of clinical governance, performance indicators, the National Institute for Clinical Excellence and the Commission for Health Improvement reflects the growing trend to an ideal of evidence-based clinical practice. It is our duty to ensure that frail older people are not excluded from these standards-raising initiatives. A systematic approach to assessment applied across settings raises the possibility of building the evidence base that is currently lacking for the health and social care of older people. Routine assessment data can be aggregated into high quality databases that can help address the dearth of evidence. This is perhaps most important in nursing homes. Aggregated assessment data from nursing homes linked to information on prescription, admission and Medicare claims in the USA have shown that the average age is very high, the residents have multiple impairments and are taking many medications.[4] Treatment for hypertension in older people with marked impairment of physical and cognitive function does not follow recommended guidelines,[5] and 26% of those with cancer who are reported to be in daily pain receive no analgesia.[6]

In certain circumstances and under certain conditions, research utilising clinical databases has been favourably compared with randomised controlled trials.[7] High quality databases created from aggregated data from routine activities such as assessment conducted in a standardised way have the potential not only for improving the monitoring of quality and outcomes of care for older people, but also of building the evidence base so sorely lacking. This applies to existing practice and to new developments such as those proposed for intermediate care services.

Conclusion

While documenting need is not the same as addressing it, there is increasing evidence that the use of systematic assessment improves quality of care.[8–10] One thing is certain, if problems are not documented, they cannot possibly be measured and if they cannot be measured, quality of care cannot be measured.

References

1   Secretary of State for Health. *Shaping the future NHS: long term planning for hospitals and related services: consultation document on the findings of the National Beds Enquiry.* London: Department of Health, 1999.

2   Zimmerman D, Karon S, Arling G, Clark B, *et al.* The development and testing of nursing home quality indicators. *Health Care Financing Rev* 1995; **16**: 107–27.

3   Morris JN, Fries BE, Mehr DR, Hawes C, *et al.* MDS Cognitive Performance Scale. *J Gerontol* 1994; **49**: M174–82.

4   Gambassi G, Landi F, Peng L, Brostrup-Jensen C, *et al.* Validity of diagnostic and drug data in standardised nursing home resident assessments: potential for geriatric pharmacoepidemiology. SAGE Study Group. Systematic Assessment of Geriatric drug use via Epidemiology. *Med Care* 1998; **36**: 167–79.

5   Gambassi G, Lapane K, Sgadari A, Landi F, *et al.* Prevalence, clinical correlates and treatment of hypertension in elderly nursing home residents. SAGE (Systematic Assessment of Geriatric drug use via Epidemiology) Study Group. *Arch Intern Med* 1998; **158**: 2377–85.

6   Bernabei R, Gambassi G, Lapane K, Landi F, *et al.* Management of pain in elderly patients with cancer. SAGE Study Group. Systematic Assessment of Geriatric drug use via Epidemiology. *JAMA* 1998; **279**: 1877–82.

7   Britton A, McPherson K, McKee M, Sanderson C, *et al.* Choosing between randomised and non-randomised studies: a systematic review. *Health Technol Assess* 1998; **2**: 1–124.

8   Phillips CD, Morris JN, Hawes C, Fries BE, *et al.* Association of the Resident Assessment Instrument (RAI) with changes in function, cognition and psychosocial status. *J Am Geriatr Soc* 1997; **45**: 986–93.

9   Mor V, Intrator O, Fries BE, Phillips C, *et al.* Changes in hospitalization associated with introducing the Resident Assessment Instrument. *J Am Geriatr Soc* 1997; **45**: 1002–10.

10 Fries BE, Hawes C, Morris JN, Phillips CD, *et al.* Effect of the National Resident Assessment Instrument on selected health conditions and problems. *J Am Geriatr Soc* 1997; **45**: 994–1001.

SECTION 4

Discussion and conclusion

11 | The National Service Framework for older people: issues and concerns voiced by healthcare professionals

Andrew Georgiou
Outcomes Programme Co-ordinator, Clinical Effectiveness and Evaluation Unit, Royal College of Physicians, London

Luna Islam
Project Co-ordinator, Clinical Effectiveness and Evaluation Unit, Royal College of Physicians, London

This chapter summarises the discussions held during the conference into the following four broad topic areas:

1 Clinical effectiveness versus cost effectiveness.
2 Accountability.
3 Resources.
4 Delivery of quality of care, the major issues of which are discussed in terms of the three phases of Donabedian's quality cycle:[1]

▌ setting standards
▌ measuring quality
▌ stimulating and implementing change.

Clinical effectiveness versus cost effectiveness

The remit of the National Institute for Clinical Excellence (NICE) and the National Service Frameworks (NSFs) reveal that the recommendations for management and treatment must take into account an evaluation of resource costs. At some point, it is likely that such constraints will conflict with clinical concerns about providing the best possible treatment for individual patients. Variations in the way health authorities around the country have analysed and allocated resources for expensive treatments have given rise to postcode prescribing, leading to unequal distribution of resources.

These issues were recurrent themes in the discussions about the roles of the NSF and NICE. **Edmund Dunstan** (Consultant Geriatrician) drew attention to the implications of thrombolysis trials in stroke that would require colossal investment in neuroradiology in every hospital in the country dealing with acute stroke. He noted that, by using a more expensive product, there is a strong implication that a cost can actually be placed on saving an extra life.

Peter Littlejohns emphasised that there is a value judgement to be made. These are issues of particular importance to NICE's Patients' Council. He stressed that there is no formula that NICE can use to determine a solution. NICE can provide advice, but it must then be debated as such. Other delegates emphasised that the NSF would be addressing a broad range of aspects of quality, including clinical effectiveness, social acceptability, equity and relevance. Cost effectiveness is a consideration, but part of the NSF's remit is to be cost neutral.

Accountability

Some of the major aspects of the new arrangements in the NHS include:

▌ the desire for increased transparency of information
▌ increased public awareness of performance, and
▌ the accountability of individuals for meeting quality standards.

These requirements create possible areas of tension between an ever-increasing scrutiny of medical practice by the media and medico-legal organisations, and corresponding concerns about the quality of information, for example, published league tables that provide only a partial picture and are often based on data that have severe limitations in how they can be interpreted. Moreover, the need to be seen to conform with guidelines and protocols may limit the clinician's scope to adapt to individual circumstances and constrain the quest for innovation and improvement.

Michael Pearson drew attention to the issue of accountability when he asked how delegates would feel if data were routinely collected and then appeared in the local press with alarming headlines. He noted that the concept of clinical governance implies that such figures may be used in that way.

Ian Philp confirmed the importance of accountability within the NSF for older people, stating that agreed standards must be precise, in important areas and deliverable – and someone must be held accountable. There is no point in writing standards unless they make a difference. One delegate reflected on a local situation where variations in outcome between hospitals had been reported. Although the variations could be explained on the basis of case mix differences between hospitals, the information nevertheless indicated that more resources were needed to deal with their problem. The data had identified an important issue requiring further investigation.

The importance of taking care in interpreting outcome data was emphasised by **Alastair Mason**. He said that health outcome indicators simply indicate a possible problem which it is worth spending some time investigating. Much measurement of quality acts as a pointer to whether there may be problems, and should not be taken to mean that there are *necessarily* problems. Public promulgation of such measurements should be accompanied by a health warning as to the limitations of the data.

Resources

Neil Walker (Director, Care and Community Services, Shaftesbury Society) stated that there would be very few people present who believed that the resources of the NHS or community care are satisfactory as they currently exist. Resourcing for the health service has long been a controversial issue. The NHS is under-resourced compared with other European countries. Government recognition of this has been highlighted by its recent commitment to increase spending. At the same time, as noted earlier, there is a powerful drive to ensure that the service is managed in the most cost efficient manner possible. Problems can arise when practitioners become concerned that changes will be implemented without the provision of adequate resources.

Concern about resources was expressed during discussion periods at each of the conference sessions. A common refrain was that there is no point in driving change unless resources are available to facilitate change and enable high quality care. **Sheila Adam** noted that the one thing likely to be the biggest block to delivering NSFs in general is having the right staff in the right place doing the right things. **Peter Millard** (Emeritus Professor of Geriatrics) made a similar point when he said that if 34% of people in residential homes are incontinent of urine, it is totally unacceptable that the staff looking after them are not trained to manage incontinence. He considers that the main cause of declining standards in hospital has been the downplaying of the basic care staff and their training.

Various speakers asserted the importance of maximising benefit within current resources. **Ian Philp** said we have to be realistic and think how we can do better with the available resources. **Sheila Adam** added that quite a lot can be done within existing resources, and should be possible in the short to medium term.

Delivering quality of care

The studies on stroke, fractured proximal femur and urinary incontinence presented at the conference encouraged discussion about important methodological issues associated with measuring the quality of care. The issues can be considered within the context of the quality cycle described by Donabedian:[1]

▌ *Phase 1*: the setting of standards.
▌ *Phase 2*: the measurement of quality in practice using the standards.
▌ *Phase 3*: the employment of change strategies to adjust practice to approximate to the standards.

Finally, practice must be measured again to ensure progress is being made towards higher standards of care.

Phase 1: setting the standards

Evidence base. There is great emphasis in the new Department of Health proposals about the need to ensure that standards are evidence-based. However, it is often difficult to relate the local situation precisely to research-based evidence. Such evidence may be based on studies carried out with differing methodologies, varying practices and differing population groups. The problems of heterogeneity are particularly pronounced when considering care for older people. These difficulties were addressed in the conference by **Carol Jagger** (Senior Lecturer) who expressed concern that the evidence base for older people is not particularly good because they are excluded from trials. She asked whether NICE will look at older people as a specific group in any of the guidelines so that there will be evidence of good practice for the care of older people. **Peter Littlejohns** replied that the identification of subgroups or risk groups will be crucial. The information is often not available, hence one of the roles of NICE is to inform the research process on this.

Finbarr Martin (Clinical Director) drew attention to the problem of finding an appropriate model of care for older people in residential and nursing homes. He noted that there is little current evidence to guide which model of care should be applied to residents of nursing homes. Care may be based on generic health workers in primary care, and may be deliverable to a high standard, but the evidence is not there.

Who defines the standards? Currently, standards are defined utilising the evidence base as far as possible, and supplemented by the considered opinion of expert and experienced clinicians. The importance of gaining input from the users must be part of the evolving framework. This point was highlighted by **Kalman Kafetz** (Consultant Physician), who asked how will the views of disabled older people – the main consumers of the services discussed – be heard? At the moment, fit older people are not good representatives because they consider themselves not to be old, so how will those who *do* need to be heard be noticed?

Definition of standards. Standards for quality can be well intentioned, but may be too imprecise for measurement purposes. Precision is crucial, but variations in practice may make definition difficult. One delegate related how one of the biggest concerns is that standards will be too broad and therefore lack meaning. It is difficult to develop protocols and standards that are deliverable.

One example of the importance of precise definitions was raised by **Ann Palmer** (Consultant in Public Health Medicine) who challenged the idea that care in a stroke unit is the standard. The four stroke units with which she is familiar are extraordinarily variable in the level of disability of patients, and the stage at which they are discharged into the community. The evidence relates to stroke *teams* not stroke *units.* **Martin Dennis** (Reader in Stroke Medicine) said that this raised an interesting issue about how to define a stroke unit. There has been a huge amount of relabelling of wards to meet local priorities in the last few years. The only way round the difficulty is to have external peer review of the unit to decide that it meets some defined criteria.

Population subgroups. Discussion on the quality of care generally tends to centre on hospital settings. The conference discussion, however, stressed the importance of other settings such as residential and nursing homes, and care in the community. **Bruno Bubna-Kasteliz** (Consultant Geriatrician) stated that, as a geriatrician, one of the things that worries him is the move into the private sector of much of the rehabilitative work that used to be carried out in the NHS, which is therefore now outside the control of the NHS. A similar point was made by another delegate who questioned whether NICE and the speakers at the conference have any interest, either currently or in the future, in what happens to people outside hospitals, particularly older people. Our most handicapped and most vulnerable people are in nursing homes. Does anyone care what happens to them?

Phase 2: the measurement of quality in practice

Process. The studies in Chapters 6, 7 and 9 highlighted the strengths and weaknesses of various process and outcome measures for assessing quality of care. The benefits of process measures are that:

▎ data are more readily collectable

▎ statistical issues are less of a problem, and

▎ the measures are not confounded by case mix, selection criteria and other variables.

These benefits were emphasised by **Anthony Rudd,** who argued that the emphasis for such a complicated disease as stroke should be on measuring the process of care. There is no need to worry whether there are enough numbers to show statistically significant results, and problems associated with the case mix can be avoided.

However, methodological problems arise, and it can be surprisingly difficult to obtain even simple data reliably, perhaps because of difficulty finding the data or of lack of documentation. This was highlighted by **Joanna Chugg** (Ward Manager) who reported that staff on the stroke unit at the Lister Hospital were surprised to learn that they did not appear to be complying with the requirement to record patients' weights – which is, in fact, carried out weekly. The auditors had difficulty locating this information, in part because of the inconsistency of where the data were recorded. Their own care pathway has now been developed, and the auditors have found it easier to locate the information.

Edmund Dunstan also focused attention on similar methodological problems related to care in residential and nursing homes when he asked whether auditors examine general practitioners' (GP) notes and records, or talk to them about patients in residential and nursing homes. A GP may have documented something which had not been put into a home's records.

Outcome. Many concerns were raised about the difficulties of using outcome measures for assessing the quality of care. Were the correct outcomes being measured? **Bruno Bubna-Kasteliz** noted that bowel incontinence may be much more of an indicator for moving from one care level to a higher one, than urinary incontinence.

Problems can arise with variability, lack of sensitivity, confounding variables and limitations in statistical power. The variability in measuring patient episodes has long been controversial, as noted by **Duncan Forsyth** (Consultant Geriatrician) who asked whether we are going to count *real* people and get away from measuring finished consultant episodes. The lack of sensitivity of measures is reflected in the time to surgery for hip fracture, as noted by **Heather Wood** (Associate Director, Strategy and Planning). She said that delay to operation using current hospital data is not an accurate measure. Recording the delay in days is distorted by time of admission, and does not give an accurate picture in *hours*.

Stroke mortality was taken as an example of how confounding variables and statistical power may render quality measures ineffective. **Jonathan Mant** explained that three main things account for variation:

- chance as indicated by confidence intervals
- case mix, and
- the quality of care.

Quality of care is probably not an easily measurable determinant of stroke mortality. The best care in stroke units can lead to, say, 15–20% reduction in deaths, but there will not be the numbers of cases required to detect that sort of variation in different systems. **Charles Wolfe** (Reader in Public Health Medicine) pointed out that stroke care is still patchy despite guidelines published over the past 12 years.

Alastair Mason mentioned asthma mortality as another example, highlighting the question of statistical power. For instance, the asthma death rate is probably useful only at a regional 2–3 million population level, certainly not at primary care group level. For indicators of the future, it will be crucial to look at the statistical power and choose sensible indicators which match the right time-scales and right geography.

Confounding variables may be hard to recognise or be outside the control of those seeking to enhance the quality of care. **Philip Millard** said that he had quite often not found any variables in the hospital to explain differences in performance in geriatric medicine. The factors which explain differences are *outside* the hospital, such as ease of discharge of longer-stay patients. He also expressed concern that case mix made outcome measures difficult to interpret. The outcomes are different for 'difficult' and 'easy' patients. One of the problems of comparing how people are rehabilitated at home is that the difficult ones always end up in the hospital.

Phase 3: stimulating and implementing change

To ensure quality improvement, the setting of standards and measuring of quality must be associated with mechanisms for stimulating change in practice. Stimulating change is particularly difficult. Problems may arise from the encumbrances of administration, unconvinced practitioners or lack of knowledge of the options for change. Many delegates addressed these issues.

There was a clear feeling that a degree of central direction is needed to drive change. The NSF and NICE are regarded as control bodies for the top-down imposition of some standards for implementation by clinicians. However, concerns were raised that these bodies may produce policy and guidance, but would not provide direction as to how change might be achieved. As **Betty Arrol** (Health Policy Advisor, Age Concern) pointed out, the problem is *how* policy and guidance are implemented. Will the NSF be clear and understandable about what the standards are and how they will be delivered, so that we do not just get 'standards for the shelf'?

Alternatively, the direction may come from clinicians. **Maria Cox** (Clinical Director) suggested that geriatricians should begin to draw the lines much more carefully about what the professionals will accept as standards. Some tight internal peer review policing needs to be started. We should look at good practice and try to spread it. **Anthony Rudd** added that at this stage we need to start imposing patterns of care upon trusts. It is no longer acceptable to allow individual clinicians to do things in their own idiosyncratic ways. Another speaker noted that there are many older people in residential and nursing homes whom geriatricians no longer look after. GPs may care for them now, but many GPs are not interested in this task. Rather than endlessly developing scales, the problem has to be addressed. No matter how sensible and sensitive the instrument is, it will be of no use if the people doing the work are not interested.

Many participants emphasised the importance of staffing, planning and education to the process of facilitating change.

Mechanisms for change. There were contrasting views about the influence of audit and standard setting in stimulating change and improving quality. **Michael Pearson** illustrated the potential benefits of standards in the management of asthma by explaining that when asthma audits started in 1990 many things were poorly done. However, over the past 10 years that audits have been running there has been a steady upward progression in the level of care as measured by the median of the results.

Standardised assessment was presented as an invaluable mechanism by which standards can be monitored and improved. **Anna Culot** (Acting Superintendent Physiotherapist) described how it took two years to persuade her professional group to take on board one assessment tool, which has made a huge difference to the quality of care that she can provide. As **Iain Carpenter** noted, one certainty is that if we do not document what we do, it cannot possibly be measured whereas, if what we do is systematically documented, care can be improved.

Reference

1   Donabedian A. *Needed research in the assessment and monitoring of the quality of medical care.* Washington: US Department of Health, Education and Welfare. National Centre for Health Services Research. DHEW Publication No (PHS) 78–3219, 1978.

12 | Measuring the quality of care for older people: positive approaches for the future

Michael Pearson
Director, Clinical Effectiveness and Evaluation Unit,
Royal College of Physicians, London

Jonathan Potter
Associate Director, Care of Older People, Clinical Effectiveness and Evaluation
Unit, Royal College of Physicians, London

The measurement and monitoring of healthcare have been important and much discussed components of NHS activity over the past two decades. Initially, the emphasis was on the monitoring of hospital activity and financial costs. The recent concentration on monitoring quality poses new and complex problems. Quality is not as easily defined or measurable as outpatient waiting lists or occupied beds. It means different things to different people, and is made up of a variety of different aspects as described in Chapter 1. The measurement and monitoring of quality will therefore be a major challenge.

The presentations and discussion outlined in preceding chapters explore many of the complex issues which relate to the methodology for measuring the quality of care. It is dependent on initially defining standards of high quality care and on selecting indicators which reflect the defined standards. This book highlights many of the difficulties associated with evidence-based standards of care for older people. Indicators have been defined for several conditions associated with older people, including urinary incontinence, stroke and fractured femur, which are useful in identifying variations in standards.

However, care must be taken in the interpretation of indicators. They point to where there may be an issue over quality of care requiring further investigation. They also require interpretation in the light of local circumstances, and should not lightly be used to make definitive statements about the quality of care in any setting. Such a distinction is of great importance as we move to an era of openness and public scrutiny.

Once standards are set and indicators chosen, there are a number of levels at which measurements can be used to monitor how closely local practice matches the standards or indicators. These are discussed below.

Data collection at local level

An infrastructure is required to maintain effective and continuing data collection at local level, but questions need to be asked about data reliability and their use for comparison between centres and settings. Locally derived data presented at the conference demonstrated many difficulties. Comparisons can be difficult for case mix reasons and if the numbers are insufficient for adequate statistical power. Concerns about the reliability and inter-rater reliability of data must also be taken into account. The studies on stroke and incontinence both indicated that the most promising way forward would be the use of process measures to evaluate aspects of the quality of healthcare.

Data collection at a higher level

The approach of collecting data at a higher level, based on hospital activity analysis, generates large amount of data that relate to the whole country. Systems are in place to ensure routine collection of data, but the question remains whether such data are sensitive enough to be of use in defining quality. Traditionally, professionals have been sceptical of data derived in such a way. The fractured femur data from the Oxford Record Linkage Study demonstrated that simple outcome parameters could be generated from such national databases, but only by taking case mix factors into account. It also demonstrated that there may be insensitivity in the data recording procedures which results in potentially useful measures, such as time to surgery, not being analysable. The results suggest that such databases are potentially a powerful source of information which should be explored further. As such, they can provide a useful indication of where services may be less than adequate and/or in need of more detailed review.

Data collection at national level

Data sets can be developed and implemented which capture specific data on a national basis. They may include information to make allowance for case mix variation between sites. Are such data sets feasible and can they be implemented on a routine basis? The evidence from the national sentinel audit for stroke indicated that such an approach is possible. The audit achieved a nationwide assessment of stroke care, and demonstrated the great variability as well as the deviations from best practice that occur around the country. Similar focused databases are being introduced for the evaluation of conditions such as myocardial infarction, diabetes and carcinoma of the lung.

Such data collection mechanisms provide the opportunity to gather reliable and acceptable nationwide information with which it will be possible to evaluate the quality of care. Standardised assessment is an extension of such targeted data collection that can greatly facilitate the documentation of care and the promotion of high quality care, and its use can be beneficial in different settings. The development of such an approach would greatly enhance the systematic assessment of older people, make care planning more consistent, and facilitate comparison, audit and research within and between care settings.

No data collection

Reliance for improving standards may be placed on training and education. The assumption is that, provided professionals are well trained and maintain lifelong professional education, they will ensure high quality care. This approach has been increasingly challenged by recent examples of failure in care. Training and education are essential elements of any programme to improve and maintain standards, but more is needed. There needs to be an element of direction and leadership to ensure the implementation of high quality care.

Conclusion

Measurement in itself will not influence the quality of care provided. Mechanisms must be in place to ensure that local practice responds to the findings of such measurement. Mechanisms for change should be in some part directive, informing and telling people what should be done, rather than leaving change purely to education and information supply. For the future, a more directive approach to practice may contribute both to ensuring higher standards nationally and to a reduction in variation throughout the country.

High quality of care for older people has rightly become a national priority. The conference on measuring the quality of care for older people described in this book provided a constructive debate and discussion of how variations and inadequacies in care could be identified. It also generated many proposals for enhancing mechanisms for measuring the quality of care. Professionals and the government have to move together in developing the methods for reliable and acceptable healthcare measurement. The conference showed that such mutual collaboration can be achieved, with the aim of improving healthcare for older people throughout the country.

Bibliography

Adams HP. The importance of the Helsingborg declaration on stroke management in Europe. *J Intern Med* 1996; **240**: 169–71.

Age Concern. *Turning your back on us: older people and the NHS*. London: Age Concern, 1999.

Audit Commission. *The coming of age: improving care services for older people*. London: Audit Commission, 1997.

Baillie SP, Furniss SS. Thrombolysis for elderly patients – which way from here? *Age Ageing* 1991; **20**: 1–2.

Bernabei R, Gambassi G, Lapane K, Landi F, *et al*. Management of pain in elderly patients with cancer. SAGE Study Group. Systematic Assessment of Geriatric drug use via Epidemiology. *JAMA* 1998; **279**: 1877–82.

Berwick DM. Continuous improvement as an ideal in healthcare. *N Engl J Med* 1989; **320**: 53–6.

Bowling A. Ageism in cardiology. *Br Med J* 1999; **319**: 1353–5.

British Geriatrics Society. *British Geriatrics Society Handbook*. London: British Geriatrics Society, 1997.

Britton A, McPherson K, McKee M, Sanderson C, *et al*. Choosing between randomised and non-randomised studies: a systematic review. *Health Technol Assess* 1998; **2**: 1–124.

Brocklehurst J, Amess M, Goldacre M, Mason A, *et al* (eds). *Health outcome indicators for urinary incontinence. Report of a working group to the Department of Health*. Oxford: National Centre for Health Outcomes Development, 1999.

Brook RH, Kosecoff JB. Commentary: competition and quality. *Health Affairs* 1988; **7**: 150–61.

Calman K, Hine D. A policy framework for commissioning cancer services. A report by the Expert Advisory Group on Cancer to the Chief Medical Officers of England and Wales. London: Department of Health, 1995.

Chief Medical Officer's Update 24. *NICE's guidance on the use of zanamivir (Relenza) for the treatment of influenza*. London: Department of Health, 1999.

Cluzeau F, Littlejohns P, Grimshaw J, Feder J, *et al*. Development and application of a generic methodology to assess the quality of clinical guidelines. *Int J Qual Healthcare* 1999; **11**: 21–8.

Davenport RJ, Dennis MS, Warlow CP. Effect of correcting outcome data for case-mix: an example from stroke medicine. *Br Med J* 1996; **312**: 1503–5.

Department of Health. *A first class service: quality in the new NHS*. London: HMSO, 1998.

Department of Health. *Population health indicators for the NHS: a consultation document*. London: Department of Health, 1993.

Department of Health. *The new NHS: modern dependable*. Cm 3807. London: HMSO, 1997.

DHSS: NHS Management Enquiry Team. *The Griffiths Report. National Health Service Management Enquiry*. London: HMSO, 1983.

Dickinson E. The quality movement. In: Mayer P, Dickinson E, Sandler M (eds). *Quality care for elderly people*. London: Chapman & Hall Medical, 1997.

Dickinson E, Brocklehurst J. *The CARE scheme: clinical audit of long-term care of elderly people.* London: Royal College of Physicians of London, 1999.

Donabedian A. The quality of care. How can it be assessed? *JAMA* 1988; **260**: 1743–8.

Donabedian A. *Needed research in the assessment and monitoring of the quality of medical care.* National Centre for Health Services Research. DHEW Publication No. (PHS) 78–3219. Washington: US Department of Health, Education and Welfare, 1978.

Fairbank J, Goldacre M, Mason A, Wilkinson E, *et al* (eds). *Fractured proximal femur. Report of a working group to the Department of Health.* Oxford: National Centre for Health Outcomes Development, 1999.

Fries BE, Hawes C, Morris JN, Phillips CD, *et al.* Effect of the National Resident Assessment Instrument on selected health conditions and problems. *J Am Geriatr Soc* 1997; **45**: 994–1001.

Gambassi G, Landi F, Peng L, Brostrup-Jensen C, *et al.* Validity of diagnostic and drug data in standardized nursing home resident assessments: potential for geriatric pharmacoepidemiology. SAGE Study Group. Systematic Assessment of Geriatric drug use via Epidemiology. *Med Care* 1998; **36**: 167–79.

Gambassi G, Lapane K, Sgadari A, Landi F, *et al.* Prevalence, clinical correlates and treatment of hypertension in elderly nursing home residents. SAGE (Systematic Assessment of Geriatric drug use via Epidemiology) Study Group. *Arch Intern Med* 1998; **158**: 2377–85.

Georgiou A. Health outcome indicators for asthma using patient-assessed impact measures. In: Pearson MG, Bucknall CE (eds). *Measuring clinical outcome in asthma: a patient-focused approach.* London: Royal College of Physicians, 1999.

Goldacre MJ, Simmons H, Henderson J, Gill LE. Trends in episode based and person based rates of admission to hospital in the Oxford Record Linkage Study area. *Br Med J* 1988; **296**: 583–5.

Health Advisory Service (HAS) 2000 report. *Not because they are old 1998.* London: HAS, 1998.

Hopkins A. *Measuring the quality of medical care.* London: Royal College of Physicians, 1990.

Intercollegiate Working Party for Stroke. *National clinical guidelines for stroke.* London: Royal College of Physicians of London, 2000.

Jarman B. *The quality of care in hospitals.* Harveian Oration. London: Royal College of Physicians of London, 1999.

Kellog international work group on the prevention of falls in the elderly. The prevention of falls in later life. *Dan Med Bull* 1987; **34** (Suppl 4): 1–24.

Littlejohns P, Cluzeau F. *Promoting the rigorous development of clinical guidelines in Europe through the creation of a common appraisal instrument.* Amsterdam: Scientific Basis For Health Services, 1997.

Mant J, Mant F, Winner S. How good is routine information? Validation of coding for acute stroke in Oxford hospitals. *Health Trends* 1989; **29**: 96–9.

Mant J, Hicks N. Detecting differences in quality of care: the sensitivity of measures of process and outcome in treating acute myocardial infarction. *Br Med J* 1995; **311**: 793–6.

Maxwell RJ. Quality assessment in health. *Br Med J* 1984; **288**: 1470–2.

McColl A, Gulliford M. *Population health outcome indicators for the NHS: a feasibility study.* London: Faculty of Public Health Medicine, 1993.

Mor V, Intrator O, Fries BE, Phillips C, *et al.* Changes in hospitalization associated with introducing the Resident Assessment Instrument. *J Am Geriatr Soc* 1997; **45**: 1002–10.

Morris JN, Fries BE, Mehr DR, Hawes C, *et al.* MDS Cognitive Performance Scale. *J Gerontol* 1994; **49**: M174–82.

Mulrow CD, Cornell JA, Herrera CR. Hypertension in the elderly. Implications and generalizability of randomized trials. *JAMA* 1994; **272**: 1932–8.

The Griffiths report. National Health Service Management Enquiry. DHSS:NHS Management Enquiry Team. London: HMSO, 1983.

Office of Population, Censuses and Surveys. *Tabular list of the classification of surgical operations and procedures* (4th revision). London: HMSO, 1990.

Oxfordshire Community Stroke Project. Incidence of stroke in Oxfordshire: first year's experience of a community stroke register. *Br Med J* 1983; **287**: 713–7.

Parry V. Time for action at a stroke. *News of the World*, 17 October 1999.

Phillips CD, Morris JN, Hawes C, Fries BE, *et al.* Association of the Resident Assessment Instrument (RAI) with changes in function, cognition and psychosocial status. *J Am Geriatr Soc* 1997; **45**: 986–93.

Rayner M, Petersen S. *European cardiovascular disease statistics.* London: British Heart Foundation, 2000.

Rudd AG, Irwin P, Rutledge Z, Lowe D, *et al.* The national sentinel audit for stroke: a tool for raising standards of care. *J R Coll Physicians Lond* 1999; **33**: 460–4.

Rudd A, Pearson MG, Georgiou A (eds). *Measuring clinical outcome in stroke (acute care).* London: Royal College of Physicians, 2000.

Rudd A, Goldacre M, Amess M, Fletcher J, *et al* (eds). *Health outcome indicators: stroke. Report of a working group to the Department of Health.* Oxford: National Centre for Health Outcomes Development, 1999.

Scally G, Donaldson LJ. The NHS's 50 Anniversary. Clinical governance and the drive for quality improvement in the new NHS. *Br Med J* 1998; **317**: 61–5.

Scottish Intercollegiate Guidelines Network (SIGN). *Criteria for appraisal for national use.* Edinburgh: SIGN, 1995.

Scottish Intercollegiate Guidelines Network. *A national clinical guideline recommended for use in Scotland by the Scottish Intercollegiate Guidelines Network (SIGN).* Edinburgh: SIGN, 1997.

Secretary of State for Health. *Modernising social services: promoting independence, improving protection, raising standards.* Cm 4169. London: HMSO, 1998.

Secretary of State for Health. *Our healthier nation: a contract for health.* Cm 4386. London: HMSO, 1998.

Secretary of State for Health. *Shaping the future NHS: long term planning for hospitals and related services: consultation document on the findings of the National Beds Enquiry.* London: HMSO, 1999.

Sikora K. Cancer survival in Britain. *Br Med J* 1999; **319**: 461–2.

Stroke module of the Cochrane database of systematic reviews. London: British Medical Journal Publishing, 1996.

Stroke Unit Trialists' Collaboration. *Organised in-patient (stroke unit) care for stroke.* (Cochrane Review). In: The Cochrane Library, Issue 4, 1999. Oxford: Software Update.

Turner-Stokes L, Turner-Stokes T, Schon K, Turner-Stokes H, *et al.* Charter for disabled people using hospitals: a completed access audit cycle. *J R Coll Physicians Lond* 2000; **34**: 185–9.

Warren MW. Care of the chronic aged sick. *Lancet* 1946; **i**: 841.

Warren MW. Geriatrics: a medical, social and economic problem. *Practitioner* 1946; **157**: 384.

Warren MW. Care of the chronic sick: a case for treating chronic sick in blocks in a general hospital. *Br Med J* 1943; **2**: 822.

Wolfe C, Beech R, Radcliffe M, Rudd AG. Stroke care in Europe. Can we learn lessons from the different ways stroke is managed in different countries? *J R Soc Health* 1995; **115**: 143–7.

Wolfe CD, Tilling K, Beech R, Rudd AG. Variations in case fatality and dependency from stroke in western and central Europe. The European BIOMED Study of Stroke Care Group. *Stroke* 1999; **30**: 350–6.

Yusuf S, Peto R, Lewis J, Collins R, *et al.* Beta blockade during and after myocardial infarction: an overview of the randomised trials. *Prog Cardiovasc Dis* 1985; **27**: 335–71.

Zanamivir for influenza. *Drug Ther Bull* 1999; **37**: 81–4.

Zimmerman D, Karon S, Arling G, Clark B, *et al.* The development and testing of nursing home quality indicators. *Health Care Financing Rev* 1995; **16**: 107–27.